The Kahlil Weston Hour

Kahlil Weston

authorHOUSE®

AuthorHouse™
1663 Liberty Drive
Bloomington, IN 47403
www.authorhouse.com
Phone: 1-800-839-8640

First published by AuthorHouse 6/14/2010

ISBN: 978-1-4520-1754-9 (e)
ISBN: 978-1-4520-1753-2 (sc)

Printed in the United States of America
Bloomington, Indiana

This book is printed on acid-free paper.

I like to dedicate this book to the two people that were Kahlil Weston fans from day one when I started this writing journey. I want to dedicate this book to Lisa Perkins and Kenyetta Mitchell. I believe in staying loyal and you two were reading me and never treated me any differently and I think it's fair. I'm thinking with common sense and not with a heavy heart.

I would like to thank the following first off I like to thank the Almighty God and Jesus Christ for their guidance and direction. I also like to thank my aunt Gearldine Weston thank you Aunt Gerl. The following goes like this Debbie Jordan and her daughters Brittany and Brandi Rowe. I also want to thank the following like this... Kendall Miller, Arthur Garrett, Antionette Ragone, Dan Petite, Akeem Felder, Mark Keller, John Chiaravolotti, Lasha Wharton, Michelle Iulucci, Elizabeth Musumeci, Angela Ferriola, Kim Jones, and Ryan Wirght. Anybody that I'm cool with and if I forgot you I'm sorry. Next time I'll give more thanks when I bring out number two and Antionette you get the next dedication. Anybody who had their nose in the air about me I got have no problem saying you get no fucking thanks from me and I say it in a polite way.

The Kahlil Weston Radio Show

(CHAPTER ONE)

Kahlil: Good Morning all y'all! This is WKJW and you're tuning into "The Kahlil Weston Radio Show". Once again we're broadcasting shit that makes regular and Sirius Satellite seem like sweet innocent teddy bears compared to the mischief we cause on the air. As you can see I got my assistant Kim Jones holding it down as my side kick and co-host.

Kim: You're the man of hour! What's your topic!

Kahlil: I decided that we're gonna do it like Morning Joe. Let's get political and personal. We're gonna dedicate this to every depressed American that's pissed off at the politicians.

Kim: Who do we start off with?

Kahlil: I got one. Let's call him the face of all the house niggas in America. My first guest is Michael. In case you don't know Michael is the chairman of the Republican national Committee.

Kim: You know people are gonna think of you as him. I thought you were better than that.

Kahlil: You think I went conservative Kim? You must've bumped your muthafuckin' head if you think I went house. Remember we have to talk proper because he's a dignitary? Michael nice to meet you.

Michael: Thanks for having me on the show. You're my kind of person and I see that you like and share my views. You remind me of a younger version of me.

Kahlil: Really?! Well this ain't Tavis Smiley my friend. On this show like the black man who's in the oval office I'm the one running the show. Now let's get down to business. Where do you think the United States is heading right now?

Michael: I like the way I see things right now. I don't approve this healthcare that Obama is trying to propose right now. It's not what America needs. It goes to show you that Obama isn't qualified to be president.

Kim: Oh you think?! I see that every Republican is trying to block this healthcare plan from going through. So you're trying to spite your face by not sending this plan through.

Kahlil: I agree! So you're saying that the man isn't qualified to be president let alone. You're really mad because a black man is in the White House and it doesn't sit well with Uncle Tom's like you.

Michael: I wouldn't consider myself Uncle Tom as you see it. It shows you how out of touch Obama is and that we are the party that's up to date on things. His plan is about raising rates for people who can barely afford what they have right now.

Kim: The man's only been in power a year. You don't understand the mess that he's inherited from your party. You don't think that you guys did enough dirt to ruin this country.

Michael: He ran a campaign talking about change and where's the change? This man pretty much made promises he can't keep. Let alone as you can see he ran a campaign off his should we say pop star status?

Kahlil: How do you expect the man to change things if Republicans like you are carrying on? Let alone you guys go that shit off in Massachusetts by getting Kennedy's seat. Getting that seat helped you block anything the president proposed.

Michael: It's not a plan. It shows you the type of robbery that the president is doing illegally. We have concerns and worry about the American people unlike this guy who we consider not understanding what people need.

Kim: So you're setting him u to take the fall. So everything he proposes every Republican is going to reject it. Let's bring up what Sen. Jim Bunning tried to do by blocking off unemployment. That was real smart on his part by trying to be bold.

Michael: You have to understand. He was all for it and he just misunderstood because his Alzheimer's disease was kicking in. he just misunderstood what was said and when he was sane he understood.

Kahlil: Oh he understood that every unemployed muthafucker in Kentucky would've went after him and try to hunted him down. He better be lucky he didn't live in West Virginia because they would've pulled out their raccoon hats and it would be Republican Season instead of Duck Season.

Michael: If there was a McCain Administration you best believe that he would've had the economy running and the fundamentals would be strong. Let alone Gov. Palin we believe would've been an excellent choice for VP.

Kim: Who?

Kahlil: You're talking about the same Governor Palin who blames Katie Couric for badgering her. The same Gov. Palin that calls herself the gun toting, moose shooting hockey mom? It's like what Mika Brzezinski said about her in her book she respects her as a working mother but as far as her views are concerned?....Welllllll!!!!!

Michael: You must be mistaken? Unlike THAT ONE we listened to what goes on and what the people need! Unlike THAT ONE where's the stability in our economy? Unlike THAT ONE the minute he resigns from his senate seat as soon as he gets a better job they have Democratic Governors selling his vacant senator's seat to the highest bidder.

Kim: Hey Kahlil didn't you put a bid in on it?

Kahlil: Yeah it was on ebay but a porn star outbid me and some guy named Ron won the bid. Let alone I finished third in the bid and the porn star finished second. You know about porn stars and politics.

Kim: Tell me about it.

Michael: I come on your show and hear people like you that are trying buy Senator seats. It shows you how crooked the Democrats are and how you want to throw a monkey wrench into politics. You know very little about it as much as our current president about what's going on in the world today.

Kim: Hey Wes! Say it like that one guy screamed when Obama was trying to speak during his prime time address once.

Kahlil: YOU LIE!

Kim: George Bush was disgusted about raising the gas prices during the summer time to $4.00 a gallon?

Kahlil: This breaking news just came in that the RNC has been running up a bill for lavish lifestyles. You know something about that?

Michael: I have no idea andd knowledge that you're talking about?

Kahlil: YOU LIE! What's this I hear that you guys spent $2,000.00 in a strip club one night.

Michael: Lie? Lie about what? It seems like a Democratic conspiracy that you're planning. We the Republicans stand firm behind our defiance in what garbage the Democrats are trying to show to the public.

Kahlil: Oh really? What is more out there right now Kim? This guy is George Dubya's personal ass licker or me having the hots for Nancy Pelosi?

Kim: You're serious? You really have a crush on Nancy Pelosi?

Kahlil: Well I think she's one hot piece of ass to be in her 70's. Man I'm gonna go to jail. Enough of that let's talk about how is it that you guys had $22 million dollars at the beginning of the year and now they're down to 10 mil. All this carrying on the Republicans do about Obama and the spending that he does and then you guys are spending on foolishness.

Michael: Well I fired one of the staffers and I'm getting a hold on the situation.

Kim: I find it pretty hypocritical how we're into a recession and remember it was the previous president that did this. Then Romney is shooting his mouth off that Obama is a one term president and I find it hard to believe let alone you're using funds illegally for your lifestyle I see why there are fat cat bankers like Obama claims. You really think that sounds pretty hypocritical?

Michael: I assure you once again I know little or nothing about the situation.

Kahlil: Tell our viewer what our special guests receives today to get back in touch with his blackness?

Kim: Today you get a weeks supply of soul food and a discount coupon to the neck chicken and waffles shop in your area.

Kahlil: By the way throw in a few free passes to a strip club of his choice. Give this house nigga the hook! Like Jay-Z says we go on to the next one.

Kim: Who's the next guest?

Kahlil: Our next guest is a former Vice Presidential Candidate and should we say has had been in a scandal of his own. This ought to be fun. Let's welcome John to the show.

John: Hi how are you?

Kim: We're good!

Kahlil: Fine thanks but I got to say what was up with the contradiction?

John: Meaning what?

Kahlil: First you make it out that you weren't having an affair and then you come clean? Come on Johnny boy you denied sexual relations with that woman.

John: I had an inappropriate relationship with Ms. Hunter!

Kim: I wonder what president I heard that from before?

John: Well I couldn't control my desires and this beautiful woman was there to fulfill my needs. She was there to comfort me when I needed it because I was lonely.

Kahlil: Lonely? I mean gosh. Your wife is fighting cancer let alone you're out there letting another chicken fly around in your chicken coup. What's this I heard that you're caught coming out of your mistress's hotel room. What's this I heard about trying to hide your face?

John: Well there is too much light in my face. I wasn't giving you my best side because if I'm gonna get caught like that I got to look good doing it.

Kim: I mean John come on. I could understand that if you were getting a divorce or your wife passed then you need to move on and get over the loss. That's pretty insensitive. Was it the Obama speech during the campaign trail when he called out the men telling them to step up to be fathers that made you feel guilty?

John: I was afraid my wife was gonna beat me up.

Kahlil: Beat you up?! Your wife is dying of cancer. You're beginning to sound like my mom. On top of that my mom is a second degree brown belt in Tae kwon doe she's more capable of whooping my ass then anyone. On top of that you try to fabricate it by getting your peoples Andrew to take the rap. At least Marion Berry had no shame in his game when he got caught smoking pot. You still love your wife?

John: I love my wife!

Kim: Your mistress says that she still loves you.

John: Like I said before I love my wife. I'm trying to be the best husband and father I can be.

Kahlil: Hey Kim can you imagine if he got elected president. A-yo! I heard that there more than just one woman. You had other side platters too is that true?

John: That isn't true. All I can tell you is that I made a terrible mistake and I let the devil tempt me into doing things I had no right to violate.

Kim: When did you decide to come clean and admit that you're the father?

Kahlil: You went on Maury Povich and they hit you with the double whammy?

John: What do you mean double whammy?

Kahlil: They hit you with the lie detector test and the paternity test. Like we don't know how Maury gets down now. It's like he's on some Jerry Springer shit now. Anyway if you were elected president each woman he had an affair with would've had their own room. From the green room to the red room to the blue room whatever ever as a special guest on our show we have a box full of condoms to protect from anymore kids outside your marriage and a paternity test the next time you get caught in another child scandal. Give him a beautiful woman to lust over as he leaves the show.

Kim: Who's our next guest Wes?

Kahlil: You'll like this one. Our next guest is Eldrick.

Kim: Eldrick?!

Kahlil: Eldrick is a golfer. He's the world's best golfer just like I call myself "The World's Greatest Writer". Welcome to the show Eldrick. We had no idea you had that much Tiger in you. Get it "Tiger"!

Eldrick: I wouldn't say I had Tiger in me. I have to admit this…I had affairs! I cheated!

Kahlil: Don't feel bad. Out got caught just feel better about the fact that you didn't get caught with any unwedded children to the mix. I have to ask were you into that kinky stuff. I mean I met a few porn stars in my life and I kissed a few but I had no idea you had rough sex. Were you into the whips and chains and stuff like that?

Eldrick: I would like to say that what I did in the past is in the past and that's between me and my wife.

Kim: Sounds like you're pleading the fifth.

Eldrick: I'm not trying to pull a Mark Fuhrman. I made mistakes and I'm doing my best to make amends with my wife.

Kahlil: You're doing the sex rehab thing. I realized along time ago that if you're an addict whether it's drugs, alcohol, etc. you're an addict. Do you find it therapeutic and something to keep you together?

Eldrick: I would say so.

Kahlil: Tell us back to that faithful night of the accident. Did you crash te truck because your wife chased you out the house with a golf club? I mean there were some sketchy things that are still murky around that night?

Eldrick: Like I said that's between me and my wife. I would like to respect my wife's privacy. You wouldn't want anybody talking about you and your terrible porn habits would you?

Kim: I have to admit Kahlil you do have a bad porn habit.

Kahlil: I make no bones about it that I love porn. I'll tell whoever and I ain't apologetic about it. You never hear me have any embarrassment that I watch porn. You heard the ol' saying ain't no shame in my game. Do you get turned on choking these girls and smacking them around when you have sex with them. I see that shit on a website and they do that shit but they spit in these girls faces.

Eldrick: You're funny! I don't believe it.

Kahlil: Seriously! Kim am I lying?

Kim He's telling the truth.

Kahlil: They really do that stuff.

Eldrick: I thought when you invited me on your radio show you're gonna talk to me about making a comeback, not go digging in my affairs.

Kahlil: Like you didn't know I'm a dirty radio dj who speaks the truth with dirty snooping skills that makes me a dirty writer.

Kim: Which brings out the character Dirty Delgado.

Kahlil: …..and that my friend is the dirty fact. Tell the cheating golfer what he gets for being on the show today.

Kim: Kahlil pays for a motel room for you for a night with any porn star of your choice. Who's your final guest Wes?

Kahlil: My final guest is Richard. Richard is from Colorado. He's on our show because he wants to have a reality television show.. So tell me Richard what the hell were you thinking when you pulled that stunt?

Richard: Well I really did think my son was in the balloon.

Kim: I find that hard to believe that you didn't know that you're son was hiding out. It was more like you're trying to put on a show. You're son pretty much gave it away.

Kahlil: It's obvious that a person of that weight that will allow a balloon to carry him like that. Have you thought about majoring in theatrics when you were in school? I saw how you had cameras videotaping and coming up with crazy experiments sounds like that you're trying to get a deal with Sci-Fi. When you did the interview rounds you had a son throwing up and he was sick and it seem like you liked the attention it drew.

Richard: Do you have kids Kahlil? So you can have no idea the fear you have as a parent.

Kahlil: Fear as a parent? You go on national television and make this phantom 9-1-1 call and run claim that you're son is missing and that he's in a balloon...so you claim. You don't know my track record I have the worse luck with women. Just for the record I have no kids.

Richard: My wife and I were concerned and I feel like the system railroaded me because of my concern.

Kim: The bad news is that your son gave away that it was an act that was the most damning evidence. He just straight ratted on y'all.

Richard: What he meant by an act was how he was trying to audition for a part in a play of his third grade class.

Kahlil: By the way you know you're wife isn't hot. What were you thinking when you married her?

Kim: She's not too pleasant on the eyes. I mean...

Kahlil: Dude you should've fought the case and let her get deported. You know how they tell you to take a dive in boxing and act like you're gonna fight the case but deep down she gets deported and divorce her and fight another wife. When you married her did you have wild turkey in you when you know...married her?

Richard: How dare you say that about my wife.

Kahlil: How dare you lie to America that your son was in that balloon knowing where he really was. Let alone you should be arrested for marrying a woman that ugly what the hell were you thinking? Kim tell our guest what he gets for showing up on the show today.

Kim: Well it's not for you it's for your wife she gets a facelift and a makeover at any place of her choosing.

Richard: Why you!!!!

Kahlil: Save the drama for Osama. This is The Kahlil Weston Radio show and this is what the fuck I do. Remember my catchphrase there's three sides to every story. Your version, their version and the truth and just remember "In Kahlil We Trust". Good Night from Voorhees!!!!!

The World's Greatest Writer

(Chapter Two)

Aaron: Let's get it on! Let's…let's get it on! Let's get it on…Let's get it on! Get it out there! Get it out there! Get it out there!

Once again the business just picked up because the words I speak roll into my direction. Ladies and gentleman let me speak it my way because I'm in no mood to be hitting women with shovels like Norman Bates. You're tuning into the drama as "The Kahlil Weston Hour" unfolds in this latest episode.

"I'm in fighting form!"

If I wasn't taken seriously it wasn't til' two weeks after my 27th birthday. Crushing my challenger by speaking the truth, and if you wanna step up to the plate feel free to get three strikes on you.

They say I need professional help well this is my therapy the writing. Just because I have attention deficit disorder and I got five murder convictions on my jacket that's crazy as hell and is a feat by itself. When I look back at my work I feel like Urkel it makes me say…

"Did I do that?"

By the time you're reading this number two will be hitting the shelf. I'll be still be the mad writer with so much porn I can shut down the Camden gun exchange. I wrote to prove myself that I set myself from the pack that I'm out to prove that I'm the heavyweight in the world of writing. There ain't no competition once the ink dries on this pad. I'm putting a stranglehold on all books until I'm finished writing what you see.

I'll tell you something that is unpredictable if people are putting bounties on my damn head. What is so amazing is how fast I did this first one and how fast "The Wes Daddy Mack Hour will be at a bookstore near you. I did it in record time...

"How fast?"

Faster than a Stephanie Swift sex scene.

"Oh!"

I know it's oh. I know I have jokes but how serious did I make them. You'll either laugh or get pissed off so this shit ain't nothing new. I never say two words about it until you bring it to my attention.

I'll be the first to admit that I should've been indicted for assault with a deadly pen.

"Get real!"

If you tell me to get a life then I'll tell you to get your eyes off this damn book. Let's clarify that before I continue the carousel ride. I'll just leave it like that.

Some things are bad habits that are hard to break. Like my will to write. When I write I get deep, disciplined and focused. All have writers have a formula. Mines is having to work on two to three chapters at a time. I finish faster when I do that.

Those who are familiar with me know how I get down and now I have to step into the limelight. I give props to those who were with me during my earlier underground writing from day one and I acknowledge you. Who knows how I'll feel after I'm done typing that shit. When my handwriting is seen you know who wrote this shit. I'm left handed and I did it. I get accustomed to the compliment that it's the best. After you hear it so many times you just get use to it. That's just how you fell after 50,011 compliments.

You got people that love your work and then you have your share of critics that want to be your critics. Now you feel like it's you against the world. As of right now the world's greatest writer is also the world's most hated writer. Now he faces a challenge and a difficult task and responding back about the new set of attacks he's under. The minute I do something the fuckin' world jumps.

Now that I became the poster child for criticism if it ain't one thing it's the muthafuckin' other. You could've swore I was a phenomenon by the way I'm getting so much attention. Nobody is me and don't ask to be me, I have a rough time being me and who needs added pressure.

Like I once said you only know parts of me but you really don't know me. I would surprise you. You read me but I give you glimpses of me through my work. I write to see what I want you to see. The world didn't make me a writer, the people made Kahlil Weston out to be a serial writer. I get the bad rap that things ain't always what it seemed.

When I do something now my name is hot just by what I speak, and spit and dig deeper into what you do. Just like I averaged 22.3 points a game in intramural basketball then I became a popular name. You score baskets and throw tantrums now the eyes are on you. I been in the spotlight since I was 18. Yeah…my team went 1-7 and yeah we sucked but there was no second-guessing who they were coming out to see. Yours truly and I couldn't disappoint the public.

At the same time while I'm at home trying to get my political views in. At 7 o'clock in the morning I turn on "Morning Joe" on MSNBC and hear what my favorite conservative Joe Scarborough has to say. Caught up in a fascination and no I'm not thinking about porn. Throw on the Tom Brady jersey with the Nike scully with the wave cap underneath it. Grab a couple of Snoopys from CVS and throw em on stage. After the Q&A is over Mika Brzezinski comes off the stage and give me a hug. Kiss her on the right cheek just to say I did and be on cloud nine. Then brag about it to my friends.

Don't get it twisted because I'm still down to earth. Like I am when I'm serious. You know when I'm serious and when I'm serious then the jokes are out the window. Now I'm in serious mode. If I didn't joke then my sense of humor would be dry.

Hey you only have one life enjoy it. You're only young once. I'm grown up now. I got plenty of playing around and felonies to commit in my books that makes me the mad writer instead of the scientist. I even learned how to master a chapter now. I learned that by the third one I wrote. I have other chapters I haven't displayed that I could've fucked around and had a triple book out. Whether you want to believe it or not I really did grow up now.

You know I branch out when I write. I write now for the love of it not because I'm in love. This is my life. This is my soap opera. This is how the drama unfolds. If I talk about killing women's husbands I was only playing. I'm a character ain't I? Once the pen drops then I'm a different character. Just an average person.

I weathered a rough storm and I get less credit and no due over shit I write. That's even as a human being. You know what I'm saying. I'm just as normal as the Sesame Street characters when they sing a long with the kids.

I see my life flash before my eyes. Are those who hated me are beginning to love me? I got too big for my own good. When I hear a 9-1-1 report then it means that Wes is in the vicinity man? That's the new words I hear if it ain't restraining order.

Have my shit under review like I'm under investigation like you want to indict me. Bite me to spite me. Like the world don't have issues but they talk about mine. Fuck that listen my readers I came to state my fuckin' claim. The world's greatest writer has been anointed and they're mad because I'm black.

That's right the best is brown. I only have fun when I talk about liking girls or just writing about it. The other shit is just some shit to make me not sound like a lovesick puppy. Now this cocksucker of a judge wants me prison. Just to say the nigger's place is down in prison.

When you're mom sell you out then you'll understand what I'm saying. It sort of motivates you to say what's on your mind. You want to know what's on my mind here's a piece of mine. I'm gonna explain my side of the story even if I have to tap myself out by explaining it and I'm tapped out.

It doesn't matter if it was about catching feelings over a girl or bombing buildings, to killing people I'm gonna speak on it. This time Wes does it the way he wants it. It's my way. My way or don't read me. It's gonna be the way I want it done. It's my book.

I want the controversy but I really want your money. I got to make it worth your entertainment. Saying shit with a swagger and boasting about it. Words can hurt harder than a fist and they could hurt badly.

When you get turned down by girls often that can hurt. When you show that sweet side of you and you get that consolation of the decent guy comment it stings. She says she has a boyfriend but she uses it in a way to not give you a try.

The words just sink in. she finds out that you didn't say what they thought you say but it's too late the damage has already been done. Just take the pill and swallow it crying a river ain't gonna make a difference. I guess it's easy for a girl to be so damn picky. They talk about what they want in a guy and when a sweet one comes along then you get over looked.

If I'm that much of a danger then how come my 2nd best friend cheerleads for the Philadelphia Eagles and she's been tolerating me for 13 years? She knows the love of my life is Shay. She knows how badly I wanted that relationship with Hollie Tucci. They were the only ones I cared for the most and she buries the both of them.

I carry the title because of the way I touch on a number of topics. I'm not afraid to take risks. When I write it'll be a whole different ballgame. You rain on me and I'll still find a way to shine on you. It's in my nature to shine on you. I get into this flow and watch me. It's fucked up ain't it? I'm totally misunderstood and a lot of muthafuckers are more fucked up than me. I write solo and stand solo in this effort.

Believe me this ain't all hype. I wasn't anticipating the sound wave how I'm being talked about. It's like you liking a girl it just sort of happened. Now when I write you know what I speak and it's sort of cool. It's a given now because the critics and the publishers are peaked with curiosity.

"Hey Wesman? You say you like the controversy. You say you like being out of control. You say you want to shed another skin? Come over hear I got something to show you."

Now that's a tease. I'm stepping into another type of zone. I feel it from my head down to the floor of my toes. The voice within me says to let it loose. Tell you how I feel and it tells me to show me what you want me to see. I'm not man enough to get me grossed out if a homo writes me a love letter.

They think I'm white but my parents are black. I may talk like I'm white but I'm still a nigga. My rep makes me out to be a psycho male but I'm probably more in a feminine, puppy dog, silly mode. I like being organized. Like this shit you're reading let's you step into me. If I want to turn you out I'll do it.

Do you feel me? Let the world see me get really looser. Just go deeper. Deeper into that zone. I like it that way. I got needs too. I like you too. You love me? Well…

"I don't love Aisha."

You feel something for me but I felt nothing for you. Sorry but you felt something I felt for your friend. Since you made it an issue to give some props then you know what I'll give them to my role model.

I spoke to my friend Antoinette once about how I look up to her husband. Yes Dan Petite is my role model. The night I confronted Antoinette about the crush it could've been worse than I anticipated but it wasn't. Just because of a lot things I can say a lot of superlatives but I can just say…

"You're O.K! Dan!"

That's why I can call myself that. I can acknowledge that shit in writing. I won't forget those and I'm black and I'm proud to admit it. So I'm saluting him.

The next time you hear me talk or drop. Just have me singled out and I get the heat. You fail to understand that I can fuckin' write. I have that gift for you to read it and give it to your friends and give them something to talk about. When it's all said and done all the sweet shit I do, I'll still get snubbed as humanitarian of the year. Oh well! Life goes on.

I'm still the dog that runs the yard. No matter what it's still my book. The true die hards know when I'm at my swiftest. Keep this in mind the world's greatest writer live in Voorhees not Camden.

There you go folks. Voorhees Twp. You are in a state of emergency. I repeat… Voorhees Twp. You are in a state of emergency. Nobody is safe and all lines are crossed. You will learn that this isn't a test and this isn't a joke. It's me y'all the wicked one who calls himself the Wes Daddy Mack.

Voorhees I like to once again welcome you to my book. I repeat my muthafuckin' book I got people on my side because they're high because they beat their case for a DWI. I'm taking it back to basic.

Kahlil Weston

Is this it? Yes it is. The pen must drop. Voorhees run for cover this is an alert. Laurel Springs this is an alert. Clementon, New Jersey this is an alert. Lindenwold, New Jersey this is an alert. This is your final warning. I repeat this is a warning. Step into my world once, once again.

I Want A Divorce

(Chapter Three)

I got a story that I want to share. I did something dumb and now I regret that I did it. I know I didn't do it for love, and it was more out of greed. After five months it made me think of the error of my judgment. It backfired in my face major. I'm not gonna lie this bitch pissed me off so bad that I wanna fuckin' choke her.

"October 15, 2005 was my nightmare!"

Let me tell you about this bitch name Kareen Antionette Lynch. Thick as hell, she had a nice ass, but she was a total snooze. I couldn't so shit with this girl. This bitch was so boring I didn't even go out on a date with her. When I go a divorce from her it was like how people felt when George Bush left office when Obama took over....

"Good Riddance!"

$5000 sounded like I sweet offer when I volunteered to be the ghost groom. I agreed to marry the bitch shame on me. This nigga I use to go to school with put me up on the offer. I thought it was a ludicrous notion when it was first presented to me. I was too gullible to understand that there was some deceit when you sold me the offer.

I didn't it for the shock value because I thought it would be a valuable experience and my chance to prove people wrong about me. I had this knock on me about me being single and how people can't picture me being married and I wanted to show them that I can be a decent person if given the chance. After a while it gets tiresome.

I'm not gonna lie and say there ain't time it hasn't bothered me. If I had it my way I would've loved to have been married at 23 or 24. I would've wanted a child around 35. Unfortunately I don't get those chances. If I'm honest about how I feel about somebody the situation blows up in my face. A guy can only take no but so much. I already have low expectations and then if a girl does like me it's a shock to me and like Lucy pulls the football from Charlie Brown it turns out to be a joke.

Looking back at it I see I married this bitch for all the wrong reasons. I knew the situation from the door that we were going to get a divorce. I really thought we could've been friends out the deal but that situation blew up in my face. It wasn't a joke when they heard I got married but underneath it I knew it was smoke and mirrors.

I remember talking to Yvonne about the situation she kept telling me it was a bad idea. I kept resisting her advice because that $5,000 was really tempting. At that point I just got fired from Aluminum Shapes and I was more worried about making rent. On top of that I let Manjou and his crew keep selling me lies that they had my best interest at heart.

I met up with her the week before the marriage and I wasn't really that blown away with her. I thought of it as a business deal. If you thought I was marrying a black girl you would've sworn you hell froze over. Me marrying a black girl? If you know me that wouldn't have been possible. Well I did. I already had that knock on me for selling out.

Deep down who I was fooling? I really couldn't see myself being with a black woman and after previous experiences I knew deep down this isn't what I wanted. I took it as I'll marry you. You pay me. I'll help you get your greencard get the divorce and we can still be friends.

Mike tried to sell me on her but I wasn't bowled over with her. She wasn't my cup of tea. A few days before we got married she called me and I told her that I'm all business into it and I have no expectations and at that time I was more into my ex-girlfriend Kim. I wasn't even in like with that girl.

The week of the wedding I began to have doubts. Yvonne and Aunt Gerl kept telling me not to do it. Yvonne thought that it was shady and tod me....
"They'll pay you the first time you might get a second but they don't have any money."

My stepdad Roshid told me that I should've gotten the money upfront before I did anything else. I weighed it and I made the mistake of trusting Mike, Kareen, and Manjou. I took a risk trusting people I didn't even know. I took their word but I had skepticism. On October 15, 2005 I went through with it. I married Kareen Lynch but I knew that eventually we were going to be exes.

I married her without getting a penny upfront. After the marriage vows were said we went to Manjou's and started filling out paperwork for her to get her greencard. I should've seen the word sucker across my face that those morons were really thinking of me. That's when the downfall took place. When I told people that I knew that I got married I think they were in shock.

I was being dead serious and I did some congrats because they were blown away. The first few days of the marriage I wore the wedding band because I wanted to know how good it felt. Just to know that I did it and I got married I wanted to believe that I wouldn't be doubted. People then try to find out who because it was a name people weren't familiar with. One nigga thought I married Kenyetta because she's the only female I been closest to and people were familiar with her so it was only natural.

The first week into the marriage that's when problems started happening. I began to see the shadiness first week. Manjou was suppose to help me get pictures for a portfolio as far as Kareen's greencard was concerned and the next minute he was on some other shit. I still didn't get paid and when I asked him what was up with the money he started dancing around the question.

When he told me that they needed to put some of her shit in my apartment I put my foot down and asked him when was I getting paid because I needed my money then this nigga started copping an attitude and was on some other shit. The conversation was so nasty that I hung up on this nigga because I seen he was on his bullshit. He tried to call me back but at that point I wasn't picking up. Then I got somebody to pressure on him and then he got shook next thing I knew this nigga pulled out and supposedly wiped his hands of me.

Kareen and I ironed out the day after the Manjou fall out. I was still down with trying to give a chance. What was the motivation?

"$5,000 was the motivation!"

So we set up an appointment to meet up with the lawyer and we managed to play nice. So when we met up with the lawyer I learned that we had to function as a couple. If we had to answer questions when INS interviewed us we had to have our shit right. I just thought ok we're married and I don't have to do shit and I thought it was easier to do stuff with her than sugar coat because our wires must've got crossed. When I got my first installment of the $5000 ($1,250) it made me believe in them. I tried to do things with her to answer the questions and that's when it got nasty.

I then understood that we had to do shit together so I tried to invite her events. The first time I asked her was like three months after we were married. At that time Tracy and I were trying to resolve our differences so I invited her to a bowling event. She agreed since she was coming down that weekend so I wanted to introduce her to Tracy so she can answer the questions. I'm putting the event together and all week long she was down with it but of course I'm Kahlil Weston so I knew bad luck was about to happen.

Around 2pm that afternoon the day of the event I asked her was she still with it and she said yes. When I asked what she was up to she said that she was in Philadelphia shopping and I'm like ok. She gave me her word that she would be there. Then four hours later that's when the excuses began to take place. She then tells me that she doesn't know now and she'lll let me know in a couple of hours can she make it.

Tracy comes around my place 8 or 8:30 that evening and I'm calling Kareen and this bitch's phone was going straight to voicemail. We waited for about an hour and we were like fuck it so we went on. Mike meets up with us down there around 9:45pm and I asked did he hear from her and he said no. 10:30pm comes around and all of a sudden Kareen finally calls. Here comes the bullshit.

She claimed she was caught in the snow on the bridge and that she couldn't make it. Now I'm pissed because I told her she was suppose to call me around 8:30 and it's 10:30 now all of a sudden it made me question was she really planning on coming. I told her that I didn't appreciate her phone going to voicemail and I was trying to get a hold of her.

I then asked her just to stop by and introduce herself to Tracy and that's it. All of a sudden she claims she was tired. That's when I took a deep breath and I asked her one last time was she coming. She said no and I just said fine and hung up. I was pretty upset because she blew the event off and I can't answer questions with INS if she blows off events.

I told Mike my displeasure about it and how she handled the situation. I told him even if she came by and stayed for 5-10 minutes I wouldn't have said shit. I told him obviously she's not that serious about getting her greencard. I looked at it as it's not my problem. She's the one that needs it not me.

Then there was a couple other events that I would invite her to and she had a different excuse. After a while a guy can only take but so much. Around Valentine's Day weekend we were suppose to double date with Mike and Kareen's cousin because Mike was interested in her cousin. I was doing it for Mike. She then pulls the event killer…

"She's not up for it tonight and she was going to take a rain check!"

Once she did that I began to question what the hell did I get myself into. I'm beginning to think did I marry a total bitch. My theory became a fact a couple of weeks later when I found out that Manjou was throwing a party and of course I knew I wasn't invited because Manjou and I had issues because how he tried to play me out over that money issue a few months before.

Mike then told me that Kareen was taking her boyfriend not that I cared because I was with Kim and that's when I stepped to her. I asked her how come she can go to Manjou's parties but the minute I try to do something with her she has a different excuse why she cant go. That's when I told her that I can't answer questions if she doesn't do anything.

I remember the one argument we had about it I straight up called her selfish and boring. At that point in time it made me start re-evaluating the arrangement. She then tries to tell me that I need to cool off and I told her go ahead run. We hung up and didn't talk for a month. I was considering divorce and just getting out of it. I really didn't give a fuck about Kareen at one point I was enjoying being a boyfriend to Kimberly. At one point Kareen was the furthest thing from my mind. It was reaching a point I didn't care if I ever heard from her.

A month later I heard from Kareen and I gave it one last try. My patience was real thin with her and she was skating on thin ice. I was still thinking about the $3,750 they still owed me. I then let it be known just give me the money, I'll help you get the greencard and we just go our separate ways. Eventually this latest sequence of events didn't last long.

Kareen tells me about the appointment we had with the lawyer in two weeks. I said fine when I asked her did she want to go bowling afterward and here was this bitch's response....

"Oh come on now! You know what the answer is going to be!"

This bitch started shooting her mouth off that it's only an arrangement and she had no interest in hanging out with me. I never asked her again my patience with her was running thin. I just wanted my money and her gone. The beginning of the end took place the week before we were scheduled to see the lawyer.

It all started when I got a new job. You know how excited you are about getting your first check well it didn't pain out that way. My license was suspended and I didn't know and my whole check had to go into getting my license restored or I wasn't going to have a job. I had no money to pay rent and I remember calling Kareen since they still owed me $3,750 and I didn't even ask her for the whole second installment I only asked for $100 so I can pay my rent and she had the nerve to tell me she'll think about it. That's when my mind was made that if she says no then I'm not seeing the lawyer.

Two days later I get a call from her and supposedly she took my request into consideration and that the answer is no. That's when I couldn't take it anymore....

"O.K. Then I guess I can't see the lawyer this weekend!"

When I said that she was acting like it was ok but I know it fucked her head up. I was dead serious too I was not going and I was about 75% sure that I wanted out. I called a few days later to ask her did she cancel and I guess she was holding out hope I would go but I wasn't budging. I guess you can say that I'm wiping my hands clean of her.

She then asked that if I wasn't getting paid then I wasn't going. That's when I said that's right and hung up on her ass. I called a couple of days after and let it be known that if I'm not getting paid then give me the divorce. I then made a sarcastic comment that it's business just like she wanted it.

The bitch called me a few days later and she tells me that she didn't come down from New York this weekend because I told her I wasn't seeing the lawyer. She then tells me the truth and comes clean about not having any money and that she was giving me a divorce. She granted me one wish I wanted the divorce and that would have the papers within a few weeks. Apparently that's the last time I heard from Kareen.

I felt the weight of the world was lifted from my shoulders. I was getting a divorce. I remember talking to Antionette on the phone when I was in the car with ex-girlfriend Kimberly. I was excited because no more Kareen. I had so much disgust for this girl that I regret marrying her.

Not that too long after that was the beginning of the end with my friendship with Mike. When Mike and I started going at it you know it had to do with this bitch. I began to question Mike's loyalty. We had a huge argument when he refused to give me Kareen's new number because I wanted to know what was up with the divorce.

Mike tried to confuse me having fantasies and I was mixing fantasy with reality. Mike pissed me off with that comment.

"WHAT FANTASY?"

The reality was that I knew I was getting a divorce from her and I had a girlfriend. I told him I wasn't attracted to her at all. Everybody knows my track record with black women especially being with them on an intimate level was an issue to me. I was beginning to chalk it up as another bad experience and I didn't like her like that. I told him that I was trying to answer questions with INS and I can't answer questions if she doesn't do shit.

He even had the nerve to ask me for the money back. That's when I told this nigga…

"How are you going to ask me for the money back? I married this bitch without getting paid upfront. I only got one payment and that she doesn't have any money to pay me now?"

That nigga stuttered up because he knew what him and those assholes were up to. I took that as a total joke that this nigga had the nerve to ask me for the money back. Had me waste my time and effort and I got bunch of lies, lips and run around. After that it was the end of me and Mike and I still don't speak to him today.

Several months after the fallout I ran into Manjou this nigga had the nerve to act like we're on some no hard feelings shit but there's bitterness because him and that bitch tried to play me. He had to audacity to give me $50 to settle but I was to the point I didn't even want his money. I want the divorce and out. We shook hand but it was also the point I didn't trust them. I found out that they went through with the proceedings and all they needed was my signature which I was eager to do.

I went to the Hall of Justice in Camden and got the divorce complaint. Supposedly the reasons for the divorce was because I moved after two weeks of marriage but the real deal was that she wasn't cooperative and too snobby. I knew the shit was true and I didn't give a fuck anymore I wanted her gone. Manjou and I went to Commerce Bank and got the divorce papers notorized.

The divorced was finalized on April 26, 2007. I felt this sense of relief it was over. I didn't make any friends but I gained three more enemies to put on my shit list.

Looking back at it doesn't mean I gave up on love. It went from it being business into an ugly mess. The only reason the muthafuckers were eager to give me the divorce was because they found another sucker for her to marry. Let the next sucker get treated like shit.

This is when you know you married a bitch she wouldn't even let you keep a wedding picture. I sure walked into that one. Good thing I got out of that one she was boring and on top of that she's not even outgoing. After she was too bitchy to give me a hundred dollars for me to pay rent and she owes me $3,750 that's when I knew she had to go. That's when I knew it wasn't going to work.

I'm still holding out hope that I'll get married. I'm still a believer bt when it comes to Kareen Lynch how did Kelly Clarkson sing it....

"NEVER AGAIN!"

Duty Calls

(CHAPTER FOUR)

Quinton: Kahlil! You got the Wes signal!

Kahlil: This looks like a job for…..

Quinton: This is a job for….

Da-na-na-na-na-na-na-na-na-na

"Wesman!"

Da-na-na-na-na-na-na-na-na-na

"Wesman!"

I'm snapping I'm going off again. I put on my cape and mask. I'm out to thwart my archenemies. The fear that I was writing a book struck them to put a gag order on themselves. You should've known that this book is my coming out party.

I sense that there's a lot of evildoers that are out to foil me again. Well I'm out and free and skipping….

"WEEEEEEE!!!!"

Skip to my lou Kahlil being cheesy as ever. I must like being corny because it's just in my system. I'm out to start some shit and get back to that reckless talking that made me want to get a reaction out of you. I'm that infamous as I take you back under the big top for the greatest show on earth as I take a bow and say without further adieu that got the show it's highest rating.

You say that you don't care what I say and you won't feel that way if I say something that piss you off and I did it on purpose. I can be playful when I retaliate to get a fuckin' button to push and I just pull that string and watch you dance like your a puppet on the string and watch you look like you sucked a dick until you hiccuped. Then you fuckin sip on some cum until you slurp up, burp up. It sounds sick but I'm talking the way I should've, would've could've and now that I'm done torturing I may still gaslight the situation just to make sure there's whimpers instead of retaliation.

I don't care who you put me against I take on all comers and I like it like that. The shit ain't been the same since I temporarily stepped out the spotlight. It's my time to go off and address the state of the issues in the world that has me thinking that I have to go out and save the bogeys from ruining the environment, it's like me being Santa Claus and having to run around the world in one day when he delivers toys on Christmas.

It's time for some carnage and I want to spread it throughout the land and you want some of me then come and get some. I don't mind it because I like a little action and I'm getting sick of watching porn and straining my dick looking at it everyday. I feel like I need to be immature about it when I speak it.

I'm sick of all the talking and I remain on gag order and I can't have a say. Well it's about that time to tell you that I'm out and I'm voicing my opinion and it's doomsday. I want some muthafucker to snitch on me and tell the fuckin' world that I got weapons of mass destruction stashed in my apartment.

Let me warn you that anybody that tried to get at me, I chewed them up spit them out and they learned that it was better for them to walk off with their penis tucked in between their legs. Just lay down and back down and if your body is on fire like the fireman says you better stop, drop, and roll. Y'all niggas better understand that this ain't Cat in the Hat Dr. Seuss book. It ain't about that I make you eat crow and your diet don't consist of green eggs and ham.

If I don't want to call a girl a bitch and I look at her in a negative and fucked up sort of way I look at you as a cuntsucker that the guy version of calling a girl a cocksucker. It's one of the many jokes that the Wesman has up his sleeve. It's me giving out the snapshot and out of the gate hnow that all bets are against me I'm going nuts thinking about it.

You have to understand that it's my job to spread that evil throughout the land. I need a reason to rip up my competition and just plain out behead them. I'm a little pissed off because I'm as political as an Al-Quida terrorist. I think you understand now. If I got to lie and cheat and steal my way through another set of ideas.

I can get low and dirty better yet I aim for hitting in the balls because the Wesman is fuckin' trying to prove that I'm the dirtiest player in the game. It's a title that fits me well. Let's stop talking about it and get down to it that now that I'm unleashed. All this talk was good but what is it if the Kahlil can't talk about the issue at hand.

You better understand that after sitting back for a while and sitting in the batcave, I thought that I was gonna retire from writing new shit but I see that I have to face the bad guys one more time. I feel like I have to step out and run my fuckin mouth and be a fuckin' egomaniac now. I couldn't see it no other way.

I tell you what since I'm being called on duty then I tell you what we can fuckin' lock horns again. I don't mind it and I fuckin' know that I'll whip the skin off of Tracy's ass that if he's open to get his ass whipped I'll give him what he deserves. We can go at it as many times as he likes it and he won't beat me.

" What's next?"

I'll tell you what's next because I'm going through another marathon and I feel like I got another run in me. I got the craftiness in me that it makes me that much more dangerous. To me it's so funny that when I got something to say that's disrespectful that they don't want to take it. Well I did it and what are you gonna do to stop me?

I guess the great ones deliver and that means it's crunch time and we have to do something that's gonna make an impact. It's like me to be conceited when I'm arrogant when I explain it. It's not like muthafuckers don't know what they got themselves into when they think they can take me on.

I'm constantly squatting on you and it seems like I'm just studying your moves and I'm thinking three to four steps ahead of you. It don't stop right there you haven't even heard my counter for your move and how it needs to be handled.

I talk a little crazy and I may be too fuckin' weird but you know if I went crazy if Monica Malpass spoke in French, I'll go crazy like I fell in love with an Italian. It seems pretty sick that I even would have love to kiss Morticia Addams. It seems pretty grossed out as you see that my mind is a little perverted but it's the skill that make me talk that recklessly. If I think Nancy Pelosi is one little hot piece of ass and she's 70 then think how my dirty mind works.

The signal must be up for me to hurt and damage some egos but I got to give my enemies some credit. They got an everything to gain and nothing to lose mentality. That's the approach I take when I go against some cocky muthafucker that thinks they got what it takes to take me on. Well you go against me it's something you couldn't imagine. It gets real intense. The problem is that I take it two to three more levels than what you anticipated. That's how serious I take it and I can get real sick about it and I mean where it would put you in tears.

If you cry then what do you expect some pity because that's indication that I fuckin' smell blood and I pretty much made the kill. I'm the predator all you were was the hunted. You thought that I was the hunted than you gravely mistaken your role. It doesn't work like that. It seems like you thought that when you made the kill on me and you really didn't all you did was get me all fired up.

That's how I'm feeling and it's pretty exciting when I can just go off and just start blurting out some crazy shit and then that's when I decide to take it another notch that's when I go for the juggular. I'm trying to go to a point tht you will sit your ass down and I shut you the fuck up. You can hang with me for just a little bit and I'll let you just to have your confidance go up but then if you keep going than that fast and furious flurry comes and it's like....

"Bang!"

You heard it and I know you felt it. It was suicide but then the spoiled sport comes out of you. Then you don't want to talk to me and you say all these mean nasty things about me and I'm like you still want to go. I might get a little bored but it seems like you still want to go. I got more in store and shit that I still haven't used yet.

I only show you the shit that you need to see and I bring out the other shit when I want to show it. All those who thought that could say that they don't have anything to say to the Wesman is just fuckin' shutting their mouths up and don't think that I just let it go and you I might've temporarily let it slide.

I don't care who's the next bad guy that wants to go against me and when you're me it doesn't matter and when I want some I come to take and I play for keeps. All you're gonna do is see my next act and make my target an issue. When I'm done throwing darts at my target and I hit the bullseye once too many times then the objective was complete.

Once I come out the night and swoop down to take on my enemies that have maniputlated the situation by making it like Kahlil was the one that's just acting out in rebellion. Well they're right to some point of view and I do it in an act of retaliation.

That suit is on and the mask is on and I hide my secret identity. Looks like a job for...

"Bookboy!"

Bookboy is back to cause a stir. Maybe I'm just two minds on the subject. Then I have to thwart my enemies somehow or someway and there's a formula I have that I keep to myself. There has to be a way to win. All the great ones dig deep down to do it.

That fire to write must still be burning inside of me. I've just been lying back, chilling for a minute and decide that I need to reintroduce myself without further adieu. The world needs to stop as I speak because it's about me now. It's like you miss me? I just feel the excitement and the hatred in the air since I decided to reappear.

I feel that magic and you just couldn't imagine it. I guess I became a victim of my own dillema since I caused so much shit that now I live in infamy. I became to infamous by the reputation that I possess and became the poster child for the bad apple that falls from the tree.

You know my words can be something that can make me want to get a reaction out of you. I cause too much of a disturbance when I get on my own little roll. I'm still carrying around my championship belt because I haven't been defeated yet. There's been number one contenders who have tried to defeat me and I always come out on top.

You just can't defeat the champ by going the distance with him. You got to knock me out and it still hasn't come yet. I took a standing eight but I don't hear the count of ten. I still have that fight in me and it hasn't been taking from me totally to say that I want to lose the title. I'm not going to be walking around with egg on my face.

I don't need to extort you but I can fuckin' destroy you and be calm about it when I do it. I know your secrets and ain't afraid to come out with them. What I know that you don't want the world to know is what I keep from you and let you know when I'm ready to tell you.

What's fucked up about the whole thing is that there is no counter for you to adjust to it. All I did was get what I wanted when I pissed you off. What's funny about the whole thing was I did it with a smile. To me it's like I went on to another subject and you're left with that taste of vinegar that you're bitterly tasting.

People would love to see me crushed. Kill the Wesman you say?! Sounds good on paper but yet to be proven and it won't happen from another man's hands because I won't allow it and that's as simple as that. It's the mother of all riddles to find a way to shut me up and destroy me and the beauty of it is that I don't have any weaknesses and I know yours but trying to find mines is like a riddle.

There must be a mystique about being a verbal killer because they just fall victim. I like to know who is the next to victim to put on my list and I like to put another one in the Weston Cemetary. They usually don't want to keep going tit for tat becuase they know it's in their best interest to take defeat.

Since you fucked with me then I'm fuckin with you. I'm fuckin' torturing you to a point that there ain't no fuckin rule to what I do. All the crying is for the fuckin' weak. I haven't shed a tear since Hollie first found out about me having feelings for her. You best believe that I'll go to your realm and defeat you that way.

It doesn't matter what game you want to fuckin' play. I get bored doing it on my own turf. I'd rather do it on someone elses' territory it's kind of fun doing it that way. Just to let you know that I don't mind getting down like that it feels kind of cute. The fact that you got beat by a cheesy person. I guess it don't sit well that a cornball pushed your button. If I don't want to be a cornball I'll go into another frame of mind.

It's the fuckin' fact that I wasn't taken that serious because of all the jokes were being hollered about me. I hear that shit I might as well call myself "Supercrazy". You put your hands on Kenyetta or Debbie then Camden County Jail might as well have a bunk waiting for me. I'm catching football numbers with 85% of it being served.

I'll fuckin tear you apart when a wild cat fuckin' rips up a zebra. I'm fuckin' going nuts thinking about a beef that gets me going. How many times do you have to learn that unless your names are Kenyetta Sharpe and Debbie Rowe that you're not safe. Well Hollie Tucci and Antoinette Ragone too. You also can add Shay Wharton to the mix. You won't get the last word in on me because it's not prohibited.

I guess some of the people have to understand that I have a job to do and it's to entertain these people. It's like I'm speaking with a megaphone in my hand. I still feel at times that I still haven't been heard enough. My shit should be a made for the big screen. I could pass for a superhero by the way I come out of nowhere and fight my enemies and I drop shit every other year just about.

I guess they thought that I jumped over the cliff and I was at the point of no return. I guess the celebration was a little too premature and I go out on my own terms. I didn't go down kicking and screaming I came out guns a blazing. I'm the captain of this ship and if it goes down then I'm sinking with the ship.

You know that I have the nickname that can make me look like a superhero. Since I'm new to the group and I have the cliche to the gig. I'm not gonna twitch my nose like a witch just to make you suffer. I got too many adversaries that I can match up with any of them.

I take on one enemy another one is waiting in the wings. I may have to take on two of them at once but it makes the plot thicken. Now the Wesman has to find a way to come through that but when the odd are against me I like it better with the odds against me because I'm the underdog and it's less pressure for me to come out on top.

I'm always in that role because I'm the hunted but I treat it like I'm still the hunter. I still feel like I'm hungry when another enemy comes out and knock me off my perch. It hasn't been done yet and it won't happen as long I'm still the man. I'm so hot tht it feels like hell ain't hot enough for me. I'm gonna go off into the night like the dark knight and find that enemy that thinks that I'm a phony caped crusader.

Now that I decided to return I feel like the showstopper needed to steal the show one more time. Nobody does it like I do asnd it's in me to do it to let you know that I say what it meant. You have to understand that it's something that's in me to speak it out and I'll scream if I can't. If I don't speak up for myself than who's gonna do it for you.

That's one of the reasons why I do it and still am going at it because they don't want you to know. They can speak but I'm not entitled to a say. Personally I don't really feel that's fair that I'm not allowed to defend myself and it's innocent until proven guilty. In my case it's guilty until proven innocent.

Believe me when it's all said and done you'll realize why the light on you just burns out and the star keeps shining in the sky!

Character of an Obsession

(CHAPTER FIVE)

Being a target of a person's affection can be flattering. Attractions can be a healthy thing because they tend to listen to what you have to say. Now I've become the target of somebody's affection. Somebody's had their eye on me. Now I'm in the role of the hunted.

As a writer I write about what I feel and what's on mind. I've written my feelings about girls and now I go from the writer to the target. It's time for me to start trading places. Now I'm somebody else's object of their affection. It's funny how the tables turn.

I go about life and now that I'm writing again, mellowing out and I'm maturing now. I'm evolving into an adult instead of still acting like a clueless teenager. I kind of got it but as I matured I began to think how sexy I am now. Maturity does that to you and you have self confidence in yourself because you think you're the shit.

You take notice in yourself but somebody else has taken notice into you. Somebody else wants you badly that's all that goes through her mind. She wants to know you. She feels like there's a challenge and what angle she needs to come at you to know you. You're the lucky individual. She had no control over her crush. The attraction totally blew her away it hit her like that. She tries to keep it under control but she just can't help it. The crush went to a major warp jump.

There was this girl named Aisha her friends called her "Muffin". I seen her at work and didn't think nothing of it. I heard she was seeing someone and little ol' me would've never thought I was the object of her affection. She looks at me but doesn't want to give it away that she likes me. She ask he girlfriends who I am and tell them how good I look.

The first time we caught eyes I never thought I would be seen like that. As I was being me she was definitely taking notice of me. It's like the girl couldn't take her eyes off me. It was like bang!! She felt it and I dropped out of the sky. It was pretty heavy on her.

I remember once coming home and having flowers dropped at my door. It was from a secret admirer. It had me thinking what the hell is going on. Am I being watched? Is this person putting her foot on the gas pedal to make a play for me? It had me guessing. What's gonna happen next! Aisha sends me the gesture but didn't want to show her face.

It seemed like everywhere I turned and went she would know my life story. She's seen me enough and now it's to a point she needs to talk to me. I think nothing of it but it's a big deal to her. She's analyzing my words and she's listening to my voice, she thinks it sounds sexy and I'm like not even aware that she likes me like that. Right now she's hiding her excitement and doesn't want to let me know there are fireworks going on in her head. I guess she's wondering when she's gonna get her chance.

Something was drawn up in her because it created a stir within herself. It was like she had this major crush on me and she had this need to shout it out to the world. Finally she had me one on one. It was like she knew me better than I knew me. It was like she was a mind reader. Usually people would get creeped out but for some odd reason it didn't feel awkward. Aisha's taking a risk diving in her feelings head first about how she feels about me.

There was this giddy she had when she got to speak to me. She said my name. The girl even knew my name is Muslim and what it meant. She knew what my hobbies are. She knows of my addiction to porn. How I play basketball to stay in shape. My issues with women and do I have a girlfriend? She noticed that I don't like to keep a beard and that I shave off the beard every fourth or fifth day. . I don't wear cologne or fragrance oils and I wear a lot of jerseys. She said she noticed that I have a lot of jerseys.

She even bought up the fact in the latter stages in my life that I like to play video games more. She says she's a video game girl herself. I said that my game is DC Universal vs. Mortal Kombat she said she likes to play that video games too. In my mind I'm saying that she doesn't necessarily need to like everything that I like. I told her that I was more of a Pacmania person. A guy my age I told her I was pretty good. She wanted to take me up on the challenge. I told her I would hold her to it. I said it with an awkward smile because I was trying to be nice.

Then she bought up how I like to write. She tells me that she's a writer herself and that's she's working on a novel herself. She wants to keep it under wraps and doesn't want to give it away. She has this excitement about writing these thoughts about me.

I'm the main character she tells me. O.K that's pretty flattering I'm the lead and what role does that play?

Aisha asked me what do I like to write about. I told her that I had my secrets and that the only one I every told my secrets to was Antionette Ragone and Kendall Miller. I don't disclose to the world everything about my little secrets. I told her when I first started this writing thing it's no different from writing a song. I also learned things from writing and I was taking a break from the writing thing for a while because I was burned out and I went through a writer's block.

It began to make me question her. She knew things about me. It made me curious because she knew that much about me I knew little about her and that was scary part. I cross paths with this individual and I think of her as a person that would be on the fly but now she wants to be the fly in the ointment in a positive way. She wanted to get my attention and be noticed.

She tells me that she's noticed me for sometime and she hadn't built up the courage to say something to me. She had to come over and say something because it was built up in her. I guess she got tired of hiding the excitement. If she saw me talking to another girl she had this look in her eye like she was jealous but wouldn't show it. It was like she had to step up her effort to get my attention.

Maybe the conversation didn't mean anything to me in the beginning but as time went on I didn't realize that she was becoming more drawn to me. Thoughts start rushing through her head. She starts fantasizing about me. What is the attraction she has for me? She says that in her head. She goes home and she goes on the computer and goes on intelius and types in my name.

She sees me again and this time she knows my age. She knows I'm 35. My relatives are my aunt and my mom. Where I lived she probably knew my address but she wanted to pick my mind and didn't want me to know about it. I was a challenge to her and she was enjoying the moment talking to me. She was caught in the moment. It was like she had me studied out.

What I thought was really crazy was that she knew I was once married. That part I couldn't believe that she knew that much about me. She even told me that she knew about the marriage only lasting 18 months and began to ask me how come we weren't married anymore. I didn't have too much to tell her because there was nothing to talk about. I then began to ask her how did she know about my marriage and she says that she asked. The way she was excited you could've swore that I had this aura about me not that I'm mad.

I'm flattered by the attention but why is she so drawn to me? I'm like a superstar in her eye. She's smitten and captivated by me. She had this crazy fascination with me.

I think of it as a two second crush it'll die down. Every time she sees me she starts studying my mood swings. The way I act she says things for me to take notice of her.

I guess she was breath taken by me. She considers the crush to be sexy to me but it's disguised as something more. It's pretty heavy and I never thought that it was serious as it was. Then again I didn't take her serious. She was just another girl to me that I knew on a hi and bye level. I didn't take her serious but she was feeling me taking me pretty strongly.

All of a sudden I'm in the middle of her little chess game. It's like a football player studying film in the middle of a game. What I like, my features, she pictures my looks in her head, she doesn't know how to approach me. She feels like she had found her soulmate, the father of her children. It was like I want him and I'm going after it.

She started having these romantic fantasies about me. Things like kissing me and probably what it would be like if we did go out on a real date. She probably had us walking down the aisle. She only knows what she feels for me in her mind but she has no idea how to read out mine.

Now she wants to put it out there and market herself for me to take notice of her. She tells people but wants to keep it under wraps about how she feels about me. She starts asking people on how to deal with me. She's doing a scouting report. Not even my personal information but just other little tidbits she can use to know how to win me. Aisha wants people to know but doesn't want to embarrass herself.

She writes little notes. She says hi! She looks at me a lot and when she looks at me she has these eyes that a burn a hole through me. Her mind was blown. She has this excitement about her whenever she knows she's probably gonna see me. She starts wearing make up to look sexier. She wears an outfit that makes me want to take notice.

She feels more like she needs to express her feelings for me by writing it down. It has me curious. I should be going to the police about me being an object of another person's affection but I didn't. She was like a helpless puppy with a silly little school girl crush. You kind of feel bad because she have all these built up feelings for me. I can't control how she felt about me but at the same time she needs to keep her behavior in check.

She starts breaking me down and brainstorming how to breakdown these thoughts to tell her how she feels about me. She takes notes jot em down. She has an idea it hits the paper right away. It's got to be worded perfectly in all ten pages on the chapter she does on me. It must be to impress me and to get her message across. She's drawn to me.

It was crazy how she would check my M.O. I didn't expect her to go out on me like that. I should be thinking that this girl is creeping me out but for some odd dark reason I'm drawn into her liking me and it's funny. I wanna push her away but I can't. She's like a helpless little puppy around me. Then if I did do that I would be hurting her feelings than I'll feel bad. It would break her heart and I don't feel like seeing someone cry because I'll feel like a heel.

It's not like I'm spewing out venom on somebody because they did something to me to warrant a response. At the same time she did nothing to me to warrant trouble. She feels this urge to express her feelings and tell me how she feels. I don't feel offended but flattered. I can't control how she feels and who am I to tell her what she writes and what she doesn't write. I been gaining her respect by the way I been handling the way she developed a crush on me. It's like catch 22 if she doesn't tell me then it'll bother her not telling me but if I don't feel the way she felt for me then it hurts her more.

I began to start putting two and two together. The flowers, the thoughts she's been telling me. The compliments she says about me that she writes down you would read in a cheesey Danielle Steel novel. Then there's this way she touches me. Feeling on my face, a little touch on my body, the sexy eye rolling with the smile and you can see the look she has all those symptoms.

There's other guys that's eyeing her but I'm the prime target. All the other guys are irrelevant. It's me that she wants and she won't settle for anything less. I'm the prize and it would satisfy her if she did win my heart and my feelings. It hurts her to a degree because it's no longer a secret I know she likes me. The problem is she knows that I know and I don't feel the way for her she does for me. I like the attention she gives me but there's only so much I want to know right now.

I kind of understand it now that she needs to express her feelings and if it's something that needs to be addressed then so be it. I don't have a problem with it. I can't return the gesture she feels because I can't feel it as of right now. When she gets around me there are these butterflies that she feels just like I feel whenever I like somebody. She would like extended time with me she thinks it increases her chances on us being an item. It wouldn't make her day it would make her week. She can't stop thinking about me.

Now it's like she's developing more respect for me as a person. The reason she feels that way is because I didn't go and blow the whole situation up and go legal on her about this growing obsession that she has on me. I wouldn't want to deprive her of that. I could get her mad and she would still find a way to forgive me. It's not like she tied me up, duct tape me and threw me in the back of a car.

It doesn't matter to her who I'm attracted to. She still feels like she has a smidgen of a shot at me. She wants to let me know that she announced her candidacy to be the next Mrs. Weston and she's in it to win it. She's guessing....Do I like her? Do I think she's cute? She's desperate for my attention and in a bizarre way I don't feel threatened about the way she's still expressing herself.

I don't know how to feel about it. It feels weird that somebody is writing about me and how they feel but in a way I don't feel threatened in any type of way. My friends think I should go the cops about this but I can't. My friends talk to her about me telling her that I'm not interested and I'm the one not saying nothing.

I finally show interest in what she has to say. Now it has me wanting to take a peak on the down low. What's all the hype about. What does she have to say. It's like I wanna read it. You should've seen the excitement on her face when I said that. I guess she has it in her head that she's wearing me down. I wanted to know what she has to say.

Her writing was like a mirror image of mine. Others see it as her losing her mind. I see it differently I'm on the inside and can understand that she's just saying how she feels. I even showed it to other people behind the scene my friends and I even struck up a conversation about it. What drew me into being curious about her in a dark way. She was more diverse than anybody I ever ran across in my lifetime.

My friends had a pow wow about it. We were left impressed. At the same time they kept their distance with her because that was between us. I don't think she would be upset about me showing it to other people because its positive attention for her.

Time went on and I'm one that's holding out she still felt like she had to be close to me. Aisha finally thinks I'm feeling her because I gave her my email and she would felt like I turned that corner me. I guess I wasn't out of her system. I still didn't feel threatened by her. I would study her and she didn't seem like she was a killer.

People don't seem to understand that attractions isn't a choice. It's something that happens to you without suspecting it. There's no getting passed it once it happens to you. You can't pick who you like it's something that can be cute or embarrassing. I wasn't upset and I should know as many times I've been rejected and laughed at I should be nicer.

I think I know how it feels because I been in her position about seriously having it bad for someone. I didn't feel like I was in a bad position that I was a character in her book being the lead. It's not like the girl held a gun to my head. She was expressing how she felt. I just can't tell her to stop liking me and I just accepted the situation for what it is.

I write the stories and it's funny how the tables turn. Now I'm the one that's being pursued and put in that position. At the same time when she expressed her feeling about how she felt the thing I respected her was the way she stayed true to herself. She kept that writer's truth to her and she stuck to her inner source that's one of the most important things you need as a writer.

At the same time she didn't take her imagination and run wild about it as far as us being an item. It wasn't like she made up true stories that we had sex or something like that and she showed respect by trying to be patient with me. If she saw me with another girl she would come over and say something stupid that didn't make any sense but just to block me off.

That's what makes this crush unique. She wanted to be in controversy and at the same time wanted to show that she was here and I was someone she wanted. She didn't care how big the odds are and I was a challenge. She had that "the little engine that could" attitude.

She's no different from me. She's passionate about things and people she liked. What I've learned is that she likes to take risks and at the same time. At one point in time it reached a point that she was truthful to me. I can say a lot of crazy things about her and she did some things that created a buzz but one thing for sure she never lied to me. When someone is that crazy about you they tell the truth. At least she didn't take me for granted.

CONVERSATION WITH MARIANNE
(SKIT)

Kahlil: I like to have a word with you for a minute!

Marianne: You can talk to me in public!......(Talking on the phone) Oh it's Kahlil!..... He's right here in front of me!....Hold on honey.

Kahlil: Alright first off I don't have anything against you because I don't know you and that goes for the same with Hollie, I don't have a grudge against her either...... (cut off)

Marianne: What are you talking about?

Kahlil: What?! I don't know what you been hearing from Sonja but stop listening to her. That stuff I say in the book it ain't nothing but black humor.

Marianne: I don't talk to Sonja I don't have a problem with you Kahlil. (On the phone) Everything is fine honey hold on.

Kahlil: That little incident in Lindenwold last year if you want to know where I was coming from I was coming from Antoinette's and I was going to a friends house.

Marianne: Oh I was just having a bad day. I was upset over that letter you wrote. (On the phone) Everything is fine honey hold on! Oh by the way Hollie said stop talking shit. Those guys over at Somerdale News I don't want you to think that I started that but I don't talk to Sonja and them anymore.

Kahlil: If you want to know the honest truth when I got fired from Phase One, I lost my place and that's when I snapped.

Marianne: I know how it feels it happened to my old man so I know how it feels to be in that position.

Kahlil: This is the end of this. Just to get the record straight. I'm not out to get you I'm not out to get Hollie. This is over....no hard feelings?!

Marianne: No hard feelings!

(Handshake)

Kahlil: By the way just for the record. One more thing I never had an issue with Phase One my issue was just with Al and Joanne that's as far as it should've gone but then Peter, Paul, and Mary had too much to say. Good night!

I like her. . .I like her not!

(Chapter Six)

Eversince I've been home a presence has had an effect on me. I'm going through a really strange zone. I've been there before but I haven't experienced this force since I had a thing for Shay.

Angela: You're talking about?

A certain young lady has caught my eye. I've entered this zone called the crush. She totally blew my mind and I'm catching giggles. It's kind of embarrassing that I like a girl so soon since I've been home from prison. Is it a crime to explain how I feel about you? I do feel a disturbance between us.

I know you have a man and I don't want to violate that ground. I don't care if we never get together but I will tell you how I feel. You're bringing things out of me that I haven't seen but people are. I'm really going through it and I don't know why.

You know the secret now. You know the crush is serious because I shot off at the mouth. I got too excited and too many people found out, and shit got....twisted around. I only said I had a crush on you, I never once said you were my girl. I have to accept responsibility because I shot off at the mouth too much and I'm sorry I put you through this.

Trying to figure you out is mind boggling. I think you know how different I am from the rest of the pack. I wanted you to take notice of that. You call me annoying and I don't want you to see me like that. You know I have good qualities in me so why do I feel the disturbance in me?

I realized how vulnerable I am to you. I get around you and you're like kryptonite around me. It's like I'm a totally different person around you. I don't really worry what people say about me but if it comes from you then it's a different story. Maybe I like you more than I realized.

You drive me nuts when you piss me off. I'm just tolerating the shit you do. You get under my skin for some odd reason and I don't know why I let you. It's having an effect on me major. I get to not being me when I get around you. I'm showing signs of being weak.

I'm not afraid to show you how vulnerable I can be around you. It's a strength that can prove I can get in touch with my feminine side. I ask myself how much would I change for you? I would say like me for being me. I need you to let me be me. If I can't do that then I'm robbing you of letting you know the real me.

I wound up liking you and I got a little more than I bargained for. When you piss me off then I know you did it for a reason. A source told me that I'm developing feelings for you.

"You are!"

I never expected that to happen. I'm really going through it and I can't believe she's probably telling the truth. Right now I'm taking whatever you say very seriously.

I tell people how bad I want you. I want you so bad it makes my blood itch. You're like an angel that dropped out of the sky. I never expected to have my feelings get caught up in it. I never expected to have feelings for you period. They just surfaced without my acknowledgment.

I guess it became evident the day you accused me of being an asshole. I wasn't really fond of the comment. I was angry when you called me that. I guess you were disturbed because I didn't speak to you. You claimed I didn't show you any attention. It's not my fault that I was having fun and your man wasn't feeling it. I guess you felt left out because I didn't say anything to you. I'm not your boyfriend so I don't know what to tell you.

Right now we're on two totally different planets. We find a way to piss each other off. You call me annoying and you couldn't be so right. Maybe it's in my vocabulary to be that way. If I wasn't picking with you I probably be getting on somebody else's nerves. I sort of watch myself so I don't have you hating my guts. I try not to annoy you that much but I can't help myself. I just need your attention at times.

I can adjust. I'm showing how much I'm trying to work it out. Something tells me you're beginning to learn how diverse I can be. Is that a good thing? You tell me! Right now I'm just trying to concentrate on the friendship.

I knew I couldn't fight the feelings I had for you because I knew my feelings would win me over sooner or later. The feelings I developed for you have impacted me in more ways than one. I wish I didn't have these feelings for you but I do. I can't deny them because I haven't had serious feelings like this since Shay.

People have warned me not to get caught up into you. They thought I was getting in way over my head. All I could hear from people is how much you love your boyfriend. All I can see is that he has something that I want. I want it bad. I was so curious I had to see if you're as that untouchable as they say you are.

Talking to you seemed fun until the crush was revealed. Being friends with you seemed normal at first. I try to keep shit on the regular but who was I fooling. The same time I was being a friend with you I was trying to intrigue you. I wanted you to see that interior part of me.

I tried to resist but this urge is making it too tempting. You finding out about the crush took a lot of wind out of my sail. I felt real pressure because I didn't know how you would view me. Hearing you say you had a boyfriend really had me in tears. I felt totally off guard. It really hurt. I was totally rattled. Developing these feelings for you also bought out the pain too.

If I ever get upset at you I don't stay mad at you for that long. I never felt the urge to hate you. I always had to find that urge to forgive you. If I do care about you I have to learn how to forgive you when I'm upset with you. I care about you too much not to hate you.

I faced that crisis that I have these strong feelings for you. It tears me apart that I have this dilemma eversince I became a company name. I still have to be me. You want me to cut down on the antics and I'm trying. I'm really doing it to prove to you that I have a decent side to me. I try to annoy you as little as I can. I still wanna be Kahlil so I kind of watch myself around the shit I do when you're around.

The moment I'll never forget is when I gave you the teddy bear. You went from being mad to delighted. I was pretty honored to brighten up your day when your day was running shitty. I bought the bear because I actually cared about you. I haven't cared about a woman that long in years. When I bought the bear from the store it had your name written all over it. When I heard you liked it I got really excited. I just wanted to surprise you and I was happy that I did.

You finding out about the crush was when my world got turned upside down. I feel like we're two totally different planets. We seem fine one day and the next day we're at each other's throats. Something just doesn't feel right. I start taking shit more seriously when I hear your opinion about something that has to do with me. I just don't feel right when I don't think straight.

When I'm at work and you're nowhere around I'm vintage Kahlil. When I get around you I go to pieces. My weakness is pretty exposed. I may act like an asshole but I don't want you to see me that way. I want you to know I do have an intelligent side to me.

I'm caught pretty deep and I never realized it. Sonja told me that I was developing feelings for you. I'd be lying if I didn't say she doesn't know what she's talking about because she knows it's true. I get a rise when you piss me off. As badly as I want to be with you, I'm being forced to make adjustments that I may or may not want to do.

When these feelings I had for you came about I never expected it. Even though you're not my girl I do care about you. I had to keep my feelings in check, especially when the cat came out the bag. It was something I had to face when I would see you return. I really missed you while you were out.

I was so concerned about you when you took that leave of absence. I was eyeing other chicks and I flirted with them but none of those girls were you. There were attractive girls out there but none of them were you. In my eye there was no other girl that caught my eye (with the exception of Antoinette) that could make my head turn.

When I first laid eyes on you, I had to get you to notice me. I wanted you to know who I was. Speaking to you that first time made me curious. You were a popular person at the job and I was a name you never heard of.

I had to run the tables to make a name for myself. Doing shit that I only know how and that's by doing the unpredictable. Being creative is the only way I know. I felt the tables running my way. My name was popping up pretty frequently so I know you're feeling who I was.

While you were out I pretty much took over the place. I quickly became a name that you couldn't forget. Once I got the name going I knew I was ready for you to notice me. While I was doing me, you were still on my mind. While you were away I began to play.

I put the crush out there because I had to do what I had to do. I put it out there because I had to show the balls. Word got out and other niggaz came out the woodworks. I wasn't worried how they felt about you; I was in it for me.

I couldn't show you Wes Daddy Mack or Dirty Delgado. I had to show you the real me. The real Kahlil Weston. I can be a decent guy if you let me. I don't want to be seen like an asshole in your eyes. You know I can be serious when I choose to.

The real Kahlil Weston just spoke up. He wants to hear what you have to say. Willing to defer to you. Proving to you that he is a sweet guy. Trying to understand you is a muthafucker. Being me in front of you is hard.

It's tough on me period. Every other day we're arguing seriously or we're playing It's pretty special when I go at it with you. I have a little fun when I go at it with you it makes it that much more special. At times you get me so mad I don't even want to talk to you but I'm still feeling your personality.

One girl interrogated me about the teddy bear I gave you. She knew about the bear and asked me who did I give it to. I wouldn't answer her. She spotted you and asked me was it you. I refused to answer the question. She said this to me….

"Look me in the eye with a straight face and say she's not the one"

I said, "I can look you in the eye with a straight face, but that other part I can't say that part you want me to say."

She seemed baffled about what I said and I told her to read between the words I said. She then understood what I told her and she realized that it was you.

When you found out about the crush it kind of put a humbling on me. I couldn't talk shit then. I have my instincts, patience, pornoes, and mental toughness to get me through this transition. I decided not to interrogate you about how you feel about me. (So in an act of friendship) I decided it wouldn't be a good idea to put pressure on you and get you to force it out of you. If I did that I'd probably lose you as a friend.

Over the past few weeks, we have improved with our communication and socializing with one another. When we fight and I look back at it I think of the reason why and I take what you said into consideration. At least arguing with you can be a classic. Usually I don't win the argument but I had to learn that's a step I had to learn if I'm gonna defer to you. I have to learn how to bite my lip to you at times. I sort of don't overdue my stay. When I want to say something and I hesitate to say it because I don't want to say the wrong thing to piss you off.

I knew being in this challenge was going to be a test. I knew it would be interesting but I got a little more than I bargained for. I should've learned shit isn't peaches and cream but I still have to show you respect. You're still a human being with feelings. I don't like to see you upset especially if I was the reason. It would bother the hell out of me.

Can you name anybody who can express how he feels about you like I can?…Do you know anybody as creative as anybody as I am?…Do you know anybody as arrogant as I am?…Then again you never met a man quite like me.

I put the crush out there because I'm letting you know what I think about you and how I feel. It'll work two ways: I'll either be a bronze skinned teddy bear or I'm a fuckin' idiot. If your man doesn't like what I said then that's his fuckin' problem. He should be grateful he still has you. I would like to say that if you were my girl but I can't say that because you're not mine.

All I am to you is a friend and nothing else. I have to separate myself from the two right now. It's a tough transition for me right now but I'm adjusting. I would love to be your little boy toy but I can't…well…out of respect for you, I can't tell you what I would like so I'll keep that part private. I'll open it if shit changes in the future.

I'm a friend first; my sentimental feelings for you have to take a backseat. I'll let everything else take care of itself on it's own. I believe that's why shit happens for a reason that's why it's the way it is. I have to let the friendship flow and let it happen if I don't build that friendship with you then hope is lost.

I never expected to like you. I had no control over that. It just happened and in a way I do feel bad that it was you. You never asked for this. I was smitten by you the day I met you. People tell me they know I like you because they see it in my eyes that I have a crush on you. Since I've been home you're the first girl I really, really liked. It's unfortunate what somebody has is something I want. Christina Aguilera talks about "What a Girl Wants" well I know what I want and I want you. The problem is that I can't have you right now that's what hurts right now. I hope you open up your eyes before its too late. You heard about the upside of my potential and I would love to take you for the ride.

I still have a life to live and a book to work on. I got to work on. This chapter and three other ones are for you whether you like me or you grow to hate me. Wes Daddy Mack didn't come out of me in this chapter and Dirty comes out in other chapters this was the personal side of Kahlil Weston. The Kahlil Weston you like when he's serious. As much as I love Shay and as much as my best friend is Tracy Clark you're one of the few if she wanted to can go deep to uncover the real Kahlil Weston.

P.S. As much as I like you and no matter how cute you are you're still not Monica Malpass.

Thanks For Nothing

(Chapter Seven)

I'm about to open up this rare side of me. To me it all started when I was born on July 16, 1974. In my eye to me my parents are Annaphine Yvonne Weston and Gearldine Josephine Weston. My father Gregory Menoken well…..

"Gregory Menoken was a sperm donor!"

I can't respect a man who can't raise his son. I can't love a father who did nothing to help the mother. As much as I can't stand Yvonne my hatred for my father runs deep. My origin runs back when I was six or less then that when I use to live in Delran. I remember when I first met him I was five and I use to call him Mr. Greg. I never knew he was my father at the time.

When I was little I use to live with my mom she started off raising me as a single parent. My dad stayed in Lawnside with his mother. My mom never turned me against him he did that to himself eventually. When I found out he was my father I never understood why he wasn't around.

When I was seven Yvonne tried to get me to bond with him. At that point in time Yvonne was going through a hard time and she sent me to stay with him for the summer at that point in time she was trying to get him to step up and be a father. I stayed with him that one night and then the next day my dad dropped me off at my aunt's hair salon in Camden. I remember that day because shit hit the fan.

My aunt use to have an apartment above the shop. My mom came up there during her lunch hour and she looked furious and I didn't understand. She took me to the car and my aunt was running out with her telling her that she would take care of me and let me stay with her. My mom didn't want to hear it. At that time I felt more comfortable being around my aunt more than I did with him so I didn't mind. It didn't matter Yvonne was so determined to make him be a father and she stuck me on him that summer anyway. I stayed with him 2/3rds of the summer. The first half of my summer with him I stayed in Lawnside with my dad at his mother's and then the half of the summer I spent with him was in a motel in Camden for a few weeks and then at my great-grandmom's. Eventually I then went to Camden with my aunt for the final month of the summer.

I was puzzled because I had no clue what was going on at the time. I didn't know where I was going to be going to school at. My aunt then told me that I was going to Bonsall School in Camden. I was eight at the time and I kind of came to the realization that I wasn't going to be staying with Yvonne for a while and that I think I'm going to be with my aunt for a while.

I remember a couple of days before Christmas in 1982 that's when I asked Yvonne the question that made me realize that I couldn't depend on my father....

"How come daddy's never around?"

I asked her that question and that's when Yvonne told me the truth about him. I came to that point that I knew he wasn't going to be there. I then believed that he didn't love me. When I would have my parent teacher conferences my aunt and my mom would always attend and he was never there. Even when I had my graduations he never attended one.

As I got older I then began to believe that I had no family on his side. At one point when I turned thirteen I started to see more of him. Well I guess the reason was because my mom was suing him for child support. Even when they only took $10 a week in child support and they detached it from his check he quit his job over it.

I remember a story that happened that started his downfall. My father had habits of taking my grandmother's car for hours and all he was suppose to do was go to the store and come right back but he would be gone two to three hours at a time. She sent him to the drug store to get her medicine and he had the car out for several hours and when he returned she had a stroke and had to go to the hospital. When he got to the hospital my Uncle Gerard and Aunt Cassandra wouldn't allow him to see her and she went into a coma and never recovered.

My grandmother gave my Uncle Gerard instructions that she didn't want to see him before she went into a coma and passed. When she died I didn't have any emotion. She didn't love me and she denounced me as a grandson. My mom would tell me that Greg wasn't my father and questioned the paternity. She left my brother Akili the car and me and my sister Saita didn't get shit.

He proved his selfishness when I was in high school. My aunt Ayo called Yvonne to let her know that my grandmother (his mother) passed. Between my dad, my Aunt Cassandra and my Uncle Gerard my grandmother left $100,000 between the three of them. If I told you what my dad did you would call it being plain selfish.

He got his share of $33,333.00 and you thought he would pay the back part of child support and instead he went and bought himself a Mercedes. It was like him saying fuck me, Akili or Saita. We don't mean shit. Once that happened I pretty much blocked him from my mind and I didn't want anything to do with him as a father. I didn't want anything to do with him period.

My father had a serious drinking problem. What was mind boggling to me was that I didn't inherit that gene from him. Not too long after the death of my grandmother my father's decline began to take motion. He really didn't know how to take care of himself really. The house he had in Lawnside that my grandmother left him he burned it to the ground. Once he lost that he was out on the streets. When that happened I didn't feel sorry for him you heard the ol' saying karma is a bitch.

My brother and my sister well we never had a relationship. Amongst the three of us I was always the outcast. Those two carried his last name Menoken but I carried Yvonne's last name. If I go by the nickname Wes then that tells you I take Weston as my last name. It sounds better anyway I think I wouldn't like to be called Kahlil Jamal Menoken. Menoken is an Indian last name that came from the Crazy Horse tribe. They descend from Menoken, South Dakota. If anybody called me Menoken I would get offended and tell them I don't go by that last name.

It didn't effect me when I was a kid that he wasn't around I didn't think about it much as a teenager. I remember once when I was 19 and he was at rock bottom and my mom told me that she ran into him and that she thought I wanted to talk to him and I felt weirded out. I was so grown that he didn't have shit to say that I wanted to hear. I didn't want to talk to him. That say he called I just remember hanging up on him.

I had my first time running into him at the PATCO speedline at Ashland. I saw him and he looked fucked up. Teeth half gone, his trench coat looked all gutted, he just looked like a straight up bum. He said hi to me and how's it going and I looked at him like who the fuck is this guy. When I got a close up look at him and I saw him I said holy shit. My eyes were wide open. I thought about him not doing shit for me as a father and I said that he's getting what he deserved. I didn't feel sorry for him the least bit.

As years went by I stuck to my guns that I didn't want anything to do with him. Then I started running across people that knew who he was. I was always known from his peers as the unknown son. I wasn't offended by thinking of myself as the unknown son. I wanted to be known as the outcast. Akili was the son that people knew about and I haven't seen Akili since I was five or six.

When I went to prison I ran across one of my father's friend and he was stunned to hear who my father was and he called me Menoken. I gave him this evil in my eye and I told him....

"That is not my name!"

He said was my father's last name and to be proud of it. I told him I can't be proud of a father who didn't raise me. I don't see him as my father and I never will. When I once ran into him he wanted to talk to me and I shunned him away. I wasn't beat for him.

I looked at my dad as a selfish man. He had bad spending habits. I know he drank a lot. Then I thought of how he didn't help Yvonne and my Aunt Gearldine had to pick up what he didn't do as a father. I had to learn that my parents are women and I had this belief that your parents are the ones that raise you. Where was he when I had birthdays, graduations, advice on girls taking me to the ballgames. Well he did take me to see the Globetrotters once. Once in my whole life his duties as a father were unacceptable.

That sequence with him buying the Mercedes didn't sit well with me. I was still holding a grudge against him for that. I didn't see him loving me as a son. I also understood that my aunt and Yvonne can't teach me everything about being a man I would have to learn that shit on my own. I just can't see myself in his shadow.

I knew very little about him like his hobbies what cars he drove. Who he was close to, his enemies and my other family members. Him teaching me how to play sports or trying to teach me how to fish. I knew that he liked to take pictures and that he was a photographer. He didn't stay long at jobs and that he was always trying to find ways to make fast money. I really didn't spend enough time to know him like that. Not even just that Yvonne stuck around to honor her responsibilities but he didn't.

I always kept trying to find that male influence or that role model. I guess I kept trying to find that father figure and that male role model. I just looked at myself like just any other urban kid in America. I always saw athletes as my role models. I guess that's what put me on to the jersey thing. Especially with the minority athletes I didn't have my father around and I had no anger towards him but just rejection.

I finally gave in and gave him a chance back in 2003. I was going through a rough period at that time. My mom was playing the restraining order game and she started getting me thrown in jail, I guess I started turning to him for my problems. At that time he was pushing the last few years of his life. He was already legally blind at the time and his health began to start declining.

We tried to repair it and it was good up for about a year. I started coming out to Lawnside and visiting him and tried to turn to him as the father I needed to be. Even so much so I even tried to have a relationship with Saita. I was going through some shit. I then began to realize that m sister was brat and that relationship went south.

My dad was staying with this old man named Mr.Crowder. I remember one Friday night meeting up with my dad and my Uncle Gerard and witnessing them smoking crack. I remember growing up that he had a drinking habit but never a drug habit. It might explain the reason why his teeth were fucked up. Drugs and Drinking and his declining health was not helping his cause and I kind of knew he wasn't going to be around that much longer.

He tried he would give me money and my Aunt Gearldine gave me some kudos for trying to give him a chance to be a father. I knew is this a guy I need to turn to? He does drugs and luckily it never got into my bloodstream. I never and hardly have a substance abuse history. I guess I can say that I was fortunate.

Then came the arrest and I had Yvonne and her little restraining order shit and then it landed me a stint in Ancora. I called my dad from Ancora and he agreed to let me use his address when I got out of jail. I tried to stay in touch with him about what was going on and I knew there was only so much he can do because he had health issues.

When I got out of jail and they reinstated my probation he let me use his address. At that time he was staying in Magnolia Glen with his significant other Pamela Scott. I only stayed with them for about three or four weeks and boy were those two made for each other. They both stayed drunk and were crazy as shit.

My dad was walking around with a cane and Pam use to stay beating his ass with his cane when they were drunk. Being in there was like trading one set of problems for another. I felt like I was walking on eggshells especially with Pam. I was trying to get my life together and I was trying to take that next step of maturity. Living with those two wasn't going to help my confidence or even my moral. She would say some stupid shit like…

"Kahlil you're a grown German Shepard you got to get the fuck out!"

I'm a grown man and I'm not a dog. The problem is that when you live with somebody and you don't have shit you're at their mercy. I did my best to stay out of the drunk whore's way. I even remember how she use to claim that she was pregnant with my father's baby. My dad is in his mid fifties and I'm 29 so I wasn't embracing that baby brother idea. It made me start assessing what kind of family was I born into. Luckily it was just the alcohol talking and she wasn't pregnant. I had to ask Pam's daughter Sade was she really pregnant because I was trying to get a feel of what I walked into.

Everything imploded that March night in 2004. I was only out of jail a few weeks at that time. I only had two outfits to work with and my mom was being an asshole and wouldn't let me get my clothes out of storage. I was going up to Labor Ready everyday working and whatever money I got I was buying clothes and getting things that I needed to get by at the time. Pam stayed trying to throw me out every other day and one day I came back shopping Pam kept harassing me and the cops were called.

Pam tells the cops that she wanted me gone and I told the cops that I was approved by probation for this address and when the officer asked her and she said yes the officer said that I had to stay there. First she was going to lay off she started telling the cops she was a good Christian woman but of course the alcohol was talking and she started her shit up again 30 seconds after the cops was gone.

That night I remember grabbing my phone and I was going to call the cops and then the bitch knocked the phone out of my hand. Then she goes on the ground, grabs my cell phone charger and starts gnawing on it like a hamster on a gnaw stick. I got on top of her and tried to get the charger out of her mouth and then my dad came in the room and started walking around like he didn't know what the hell was going on.

"Alright! Break it up in here!"

All of a sudden that nigga cocked his fist back and like in the old Batman TV series…

"POWWWWW!"

He hit me in the eye. I was dazed for a split second he then tried to grab me by my neck and I got out of it and we wrestled and I landed on top of him and just started punching him in the face. I hit him three straight face shots and they must've totally stunned him because after that he had no fight. I hit him three or four straight solid shots when he was totally defensless.

Pam was on my leg biting my right thigh. I had a bite mark and I think she's trying to give me rabies. Then she had my nuts trying to squeeze them hard and I got free of her and went to the phone and called the cops. Thirty seconds later the same cop that dealt with the situation came back in and then Pam tried to play the innocent victim.

"Oh my god look how he went crazy! Look what he did to his father!" she cried.

When he came out the room my dad's eye was closed and his lip was busted and blood was leaking from his mouth. The cop saw hi and arrested me with simple assault. We all got charged he did, I did, Pam too. I showed the cop the bite mark on my leg. Just to avoid going to jail the cop asked me did I have a place to stay and I told him I had a friend I Camden and I went to Tracy's that evening.

That next day I had to check into the homeless shelter in Camden and my case manager had to verify that was the last address and I remember those two nim nods were talking shit and of course they were drunk as shit. At that point in time I considered it as me turning the corner and that he would never have another chance. He had his second chance to be a father and he blew it.

I ten proceeded to move on and I didn't look back. The charges were eventually dropped and I even found an apartment in Hi-Nella. I even ran into one of my dad and Pam's neighbor in Magnolia Glen and I told her that I got my own place now and that he's not welcomed over and that we're back to square one. I wanted nothing to do with him and that I was through with him. So if he needs a place to stay don't come knocking at my door because I can't help you.

The last time I saw him physically alive was around Christmas of 2004. It was in the laundry mat in Stratford. He tried to shake my hand and say happy holidays but I refused. I then was arrogant towards him and told him did he remember what I did to him. He seemed scared and I said that I wasn't going to beat him up again because Pam did a good job of doing that. I walked away but I couldn't leave without getting a shot on Pam and calling her a drunk whore.

A year and half later in May of 2006 was when I got that call from Tracy and he told me that he ran into my Uncle Gerard and that he was diagnosed with cancer and he's not doing to well. He told me that he was in the veteran's hospital in Philly and Trace asked me was I going to see him and I told him I would give the information to Yvonne. He then asked me was I going to see him.

"Yvonne can go and see him but I'm not interested," I said.

I meant that shit. Yvonne went and saw him in the hospital and she said that he was deteriorating and I hardly batted an eyelash. Then she told him that I wasn't coming and this is the closest he was going to get from a visit from me. I ran across a few of his friends who knew me and I saw Pam and they asked me to go and see him once again I told them I'm not interested.

The day it went down was like a blur. June 3rd, 2006 was the day he passed. His body was cremated and there was a memorial service for him two weeks later and I didn't attend that. I saw my Uncle Gerard later that summer and he asked me why I didn't attend and I said I didn't know him and he did nothing for me as a father.

All I can say is this.....

"Greg I'll think of what you did for me as a father and I know to do the opposite!"

Get the Facts Straight

(Chapter Eight)

Alright enough of all the nonsense and what you think you heard and all the bullshit that is surrounded about what you think what you heard. About a statement that was supposedly claimed that came out of my mouth about shit that got twisted up and some shit that never was.

This is my version of the story to tell you what I never said and it's pretty clear to me that you guys know it was too juicy because of the name. I heard that nonsense while I had to smell that bullshit. You made it perfectly obvious that you're listening to your sister's misconstrued sentence. You and your sister have no idea what the hell you're talking about or you're trying to get attention because if you are you're certainly barking up the wrong tree.

Here's my side of the story about how the shit really went down. Yeah I was working trash at Voorhees Public Works through Labor Ready and the trash truck stopped by Kendra Colucci's house and this is how the conversation really went down.

"Is Kendra here?" I asked.

"She's at work!" her sister answered.

"Oh! O.K. Tell her Kahlil said hello," I said

"Um! O.K!" her sister said.

That was the end of it or so I thought. A couple of hours later I got back to Labor Ready then Joe gave me this bullshit.

"You're not allowed back at Voorhees Public Works," he says.

I asked, "For what?"

Joe then asked me, "Did you make a comment that you slept with somebody's sister?"

I answered, "Hell no!"

"You didn't say that?" he asked.

"No I didn't say that why would I say some stupid shit like that?!" I said getting upset.

I was pissed off to a point that I fuckin' was gonna go down to Voorhees Public Works and tell them to get that shit straight because that shit didn't come out of my mouth.

I didn't realize how serious that I was being called out about some shit that I didn't say until Ryan called me that night and asked me did I say that shit and I told him in plain simple term...

"HELL NO!"

I guess Kendra had to find somebody to say that they slept with her. Who knows it may be a story that she made up because she's not even my type and besides that she's too...well how to say it...

"BIG!"

I'm too little for her and beside that she drown me and she how to say it is so...

"Not my type!'

I'd rather jerk off to 100 Mary Carey XXX tapes before I ever sleep with her. Better yet...

"I'd rather say I have a crush on Nancy Pelosi and jerk off to her picture of her if she came out with lingerie calendar..."

Before I ever say that I slept with you. That goes double for your bitch of a sister for saying that bullshit that she had you buy into that phantom story. How many lies are gonna come out of all you muthafuckers at Phase One that has anything to do with me and make it seem like I get trash.

"How did it go down Wes?"

The legend has it that supposedly I went up to Kendra's 10,000 lb. sister and said that I went up to her and boasted about sleeping with her. I like to really know when, where, and how did it happen. Let's see I remember falling in love with an Italian girl...

"Hollie!"

Now if I wasn't in love with Hollie and if she was on the market then it would be....

"Antoinette!"

I remember kissing an Italian girl on the mouth and it was...

"Angela!"

Sorry I got no memory of sleeping with Kendra Colucci. I would have to dick sterilized the day I did the deed with her. If I did my dick would get crushed. See she had to buy her sister's side and they both decided to run with it and the Wesman decided to come back and set the record straight and clarify that there was no way in hell she could never have my child.

Matter fact I'll have sex Marianne Tucci before I ever and I mean...

"EVER!"

The girl isn't even that good looking like that and she's too heavy to wear a thong. The thought of it makes me wanna fuckin puke. Besides that she needs to know that is a total sack of shit.

(Imitating Kendra)

Kahlil! I know you didn't say it. I'm just following behind everybody else. My sister was lying and I know you said hello. I was just saying that shit just to prove that I'm not a virgin. I just believe my sister because we both came up with a lie to make you look worse. It's just that I got fuckin' issues.

I take it as some shit that I know for a fact that I didn't say and she wants to score some points. My dick is too small and she's too big. All black men aren't big and if I did I like to know was I drunk when this happen? Better yet did it happen in my dream?

I even heard that Sonja tried to tell Kendra to call the police.

"CALL THE POLICE FOR WHAT?"

What's this now you can't say hi and they swore up and down that you say you had sex. On my goodness that must be one of the dumbest things I heard about me that isn't true since there was this asshole that said to me once and get this....

"Well I don't think you and I should talk anymore because me and my roommate think you're gay!"

Lets see! The only ones who buy that shit is Kendra and any of her dumb friends and her stupid sister if they believe that.

They say that I slept with Kendra Colucci? Yeah and monkeys fly out of my butt. As far as the Wesman is concerned it's a closed subject.

"You feel what the Wes Daddy Mack is saying?!"

"I feel you daddy!"

The bitch wants to believe her sister and I consider it me being called out. Now the issue has the nail in the coffin.

Now I have another story to address. It has to do with Mary Tomasetti. Yeah I said it! More of the how to say it...

"Set of lies that's pretty much a sack of shit!"

Yeah I called her house and this is how it went down. I called her house and you know how you haven't talked to anybody in a while and you're in beatsville well that's how I felt. So I called for Debbie. I haven't spoken to Debbie in the pass couple of years so I decided to give her a call. Luckily Debbie did answer the phone but she said she was going out and give her a call the next day and I told her that I don't know if it's a good idea because I don't think your mom likes me too much.

She asked to just call back tomorrow and I said I'll see. The next day I called for Debbie again and this time Mary picked up the phone and my voice was horse that day and I asked for Debbie. Here's Mary bellowing....

"Who is this?"

I said, "Wes!"

She said, "Who?"

I answered it again, "Wes"

Then she said, "What Lance!"

I said to her once again, "My name is Wes!"

Then Mary had the nerve to put some nigga on the phone and he started talking a bunch of gibberish. I just went like...

"Uhhhhh!!!!"

I hung up the phone and my man tony was right there when I did it. Thirty seconds later Mary called me back and I fooled her with voicemail and I could picture her saying Kahlil over and over again when I kept acting like I couldn't hear her. A couple minutes later the beeper on my message went off that I had a new message and I went to it. Here's Mary going off on my voicemail....

"Kahlil! I know it's you....."

As soon as she said that I just deleted the message and all of a sudden Mary called me again and I gave her the voicemail and rejected the call. She just continued to blow up my phone and then I decided to go down the street and went to Ryan's and then I showed Ryan how Mary was blowing up my phone trying to get her words off on me and I just didn't feel like going off and getting in some shit so I just kept pressing the voicemail.

Ryan looked at my missed calls and Mary was even stooping so low she had to even restricted the number so she wouldn't think I knew it was her. Finally Ryan took the call on my cell phone and he started playing dumb and me and Dwayne started laughing. I could hear Mary screaming on my phone...

"Hello!" Ryan said.

"Put Kahlil Weston on the phone!" Mary exclaimed.

"Who?" Ryan said.

"Don't play dumb with me you know who Kahlil Weston is he called for my daughter Debbie," Mary cried.

Ryan even started laughing and he handed me the phone and I just disconnected the call.

Ryan said, "It sounded like it was Mary."

"It was," I told him.

"She just started rambling some shit that Debbie had a Puerto Rican boyfriend and that her boyfriend is coming after you," Ryan said.

I was taking it as a bunch of nothing. Because to me that's all it was. I just looked at it as her buying into the hype and she saw me as the enemy and I never looked at her in that sort of way. Mary blew up my phone that day she called me more times that day alone than I might've ever called her period.

I had like twenty calls from her that day and then after Ryan, Dwayne and I had our little laugh Ryan gave me a ride out to Antoinette's and I was in LaCascata talking with her and Dan and I showed Antoinette and Dan the number to my calls received and my calls missed. God as my witness Mary called me left and right that day.

Antoinette knew that and try to school me on how badly Phase One had it out for me when I shitted on them years ago. I just took Antoinette's advice and don't feed into it. It was hard but I knew Mary was gonna flip the script and act like I was the one calling her and this time I had proof to back it up that I wasn't the ridiculous one like everybody tries to make me out to be.

Ryan called me the day that whole me sleeping with Kendra lie came out he told me how Mary started lying and telling everybody that I was calling her all day that Saturday and Ryan knew it was a big fat lie. We were like yeah O.K. Lying her ass off and Mary better realize that we're in the Y2K.

To be honest about it Mary can run around and tell people that want to listen to her that I was calling her left and right that evening but she knows she's trying to find away to make me look like I was the one with the loose screw but I had the calls and Ryan was a witness so he knew is a bunch of crap.

Then I tried to approach Kendra about what I really said and the dumb bitch actually believes that I said it. Here's her fuckin' words...

"I believe my sister!"

Then I forgot that Kendra was never that smart anyway and she did the smart thing by not trying to come at me physically because of the way I bullied her other co-workers and co-conspirators in the past she thought twice before looking the devil in her eyes and I tried to convince her that I didn't say that.

It's always like a woman to lie and be deceitful and when you put them out there they feel small. All they got to do is ask Sonja and Joanne to Al Valentine and anybody else that I laid to rest that worked at Phase One. We can play chess because I don't play checkers; I'd rather put those who consider me the enemy that I looked at them as non-enemies to put them in checkmate.

I get my high when I can go off and make others eat their shit and remember Parts for Imports pays me now not Phase One. I got a job that pays me unlike those fuck ups at Phase One. After all these years I like seeing them sink.

This is how sorry and stupid they are. They lowered their rates to $6.00/ hour that's only a shade above minimum wage. They're only filling in half the seats now and their staff is crumbling and before you know it they'll be tumbling down like the bridges in London. Because of who I am and if it's something negative they sit their licking their chops wondering what can they talk about that has to do with lil ol' me.

It seems like no matter how many times a lie comes out of somebody's mouth. No matter if I still tell the truth there's a way to make me look like I'm the liar. No matter who I'm put up against I have to go that extra mile to keep them at bay and it's still more shit. There's always someone new or something that has to be made up and I'm saying how?

Jay Johnson even said that he didn't believe that I said I slept with that girl. Beside that Kendra's not even my type, not even my like, hell no she doesn't do nothing for me. Like Jay said there's two side to every story and it's not even fair that I didn't get to tell my side but one side was heard and that's the only side that counts before I can speak.

Well I did speak and as far as I'm concerned the whole rumor about Kahlil Weston sleeping with Kendra Colucci never happened, it never will and basically she can watch that fuckin' show that used to come on HBO called Dream On because she'll never sleep with me in this lifetime. That goes double for her lying ass sister.

As far as Mary Tomasetti is concerned stop lying to muthafuckers that I called her house twenty times that day. She needs to clarify her facts because when you spoke on my phone you spoke to Ryan and we let you run your mouth and lie. I called for Debbie not you and I don't need to say my name is Lance it's Wes to you. It ain't Kahlil no more and don't you dare say I'm a liar because Ryan can back that story and if I need to pull out the records for the amount of calls you made to me that one day in the merry merry month of May I can take you by surprise.

I pretty much said what I had to say and you can feel what I said and I don't care who gets mad or what you think because eventually you get karma. That fuckin' place is already going downhill so I look back and see you guys fall flat on your face.

I'M FUCKIN TIRED OF HEARING THE LIES! I WANT TO MAKE IT CLEAR STOP LISTENING TO WHAT THESE FUCKIN PEOPLE SAY ABOUT ME. Y'ALL NEED TO STOP LYING AND KEEP TALKING SHIT ABOUT ME.

LET ME MAKE THIS CLEAR LIKE I TOLD PEOPLE OVER AND OVER AGAIN MY BEEF WAS WITH AL AND JOANNE BUT EVERYBODY WANTS TO ADD THEIR TWO PENNIES IN THE MIDDLE OF SHIT THAT AIN'T GOT NOTHING TO DO WITH THEM. STOP ACTING LIKE A BUNCH OF BABIES AND SAY WHAT REALLY HAPPENED AND MAKE IT LOOK LIKE IT WAS ME.

PLAIN AND SIMPLE! FUCK AL VALENTINE! FUCK JOANNA LENTZ! FUCK ANYBODY ELSE WHO'S BEEN BAD MOUTHING ME. IF YOU DON'T LIKE WHAT I SAID WELL FUCK YOU TOO. TO YOUR MOMMA AND ANYBODY ELSE WHO HAS A GRUDGE AGAINST KAHLIL.

LIKE I TOLD MARIANNE TUCCI IT SEEM LIKE EVERYBODY HAD SOMETHING TO SAY AND IF IT DIDN'T INVOLVE YOU THEN DON'T SAY SHIT. JUST STOP RUNNING YOUR MOUTH BECAUSE HALF OF Y'ALL ARE INJECTING YOURSELVES IN SHIT THAT AIN'T NOTHING TO DO WITH YOU. STICK YOUR HAND IN THE SNAKEPIT IT'S A MATTER OF TIME BEFORE THE ANACONDA STRIKES.

"JUST SHUT YOUR FUCKIN MOUTHS!"

Beheaded

(Chapter Nine)

I got five American hostages and some Turkish truck drivers that I kidnapped on the way to the secret location. Wes Zarquawi is out and ready to take up for my Al-Queda people. The president didn't want to meet my demands and he wanted Saddaam hunted down.

I can get wounded and I still feel like I'm Superman. I feel so strong and I got wounded and kryptonite couldn't stop me. I'm in a killers mentality type of mind and I want to kidnap the Americans that took over Iraq. Now I'm an Iraqi rebel who's still fighting the good war for Al-Quida.

Now I got Osama two waying me to kill some of the Americans that I kidnapped and he gave me the orders to kill them on the Al-Jazeera network and let their families feel their pain. These Americans think it's a joke that I'm gonna lay down and play dead for these weaklings. Well America wants to roll into the middle east they better understand that this isn't 1991.

The president couldn't catch us so he did the next best thing. Wasn't he suppose to be coming after Al-Queda for hijacking the planes and we flew them into the towers. We got the Pentagon in D.C. and we would've got the White House if the passengers on the plane didn't try to play hero. We decide that we don't like Americans and you should've never voted another Bush back in the office.

Since the day of 9/11 we have been in a war with America and we don't like the way America let Bush back in office. They heard us respond the only way we know how. We didn't want them coming out to Iraq but they did it anyway. They couldn't catch us so they had to catch Sadaam. It takes more than catching the Iraqi leader to intimidate us.

One day we decide we want to kill somebody and we want them to look in horror that if you come to invade Iraq. We saw this guy supposedly looking for work and he said his name was Nick. Me and my boys snatched him up and we took him as our prisoner. We tied him up and we chained him and we fed him vinegar and bread.

We made him wear an orange jumpsuit to make him feel like he's our prisoner since the American soldiers were making our Iraqi people play the gay game in Albu Gharib Prison. They making them stack on top of each other naked like a stack at the International House of Pancakes. They better understand that we don't play the gay game.

I made a two way call to bin Laden about how he wanted to handled and he said handle your business any way you know how. He felt like you have to kill him another way and don't use the regular tactics you use when you kill him. He did tell me to televise it so the Americans know what they're getting in.

"I want him dead!" bin Laden demanded.

"You read my mind very well and I intend on doing that," I exclaimed.

"We can't crash another plane into the building. We're gonna break somebody's heart if we kill this guy. What makes it more meaningful is that it's an American family," bin Laden said.

"It'll be taken care of in all due time," I said.

"How are you gonna kill him?" he asked.

"You'll have to see on Al-Jazeera network. I'll make sure that it makes the Internet," I said sheepishly.

"Allah Ahkbar!" he exclaimed.

We signed off and I had pulled out a knife and decided that I was gonna slit his throat but how far would I take it. I had to meet bin Laden's demand and kill him on television.

I rounded up the clique and we all threw on masks and put on our Arab gear and we shackled him up. Put the cuffs on him and decided to let him get his air play before we did out act of treachery. We gathered behind him and let him speak his name and where he was from. He said he was Pennsylvania and that he came to Iraq looking for work.

As my Al-Queda mates looked on we watched him give his profile with his jumpsuit on and his beard looking rugged on him. That's when I looked over to my other running buddies and they could see it in my eyes that I wanted to finish him.

I pulled out a paper after he was done gibbering and I was like....

"Allah Ahkbar!"

That's when I pulled out a knife and decided that it was time to put him out of his misery and start the suffering of a family to grieve over their missing son. I didn't feel a conscience when I did it. Put the knife up to his throat and began to go for his throat and you could hear him gasp for air and I cut off his windpipe. I didn't want to stop there.

I made it a point that when I attack you with words I want to finish you like they use fatalities in Mortal Kombat. I began to hear him gasp for air and scream and I still was slicing away at his throat. Then I saw blood gushing around his neck and I was enjoying it. I kept going away and my comrades looked on.

Then his head came completely off. I showed his head and the rest of his body layed flat on the floor without his head. I knew he was dead. That's when I sung my praises to Allah about my latest acts. After I flashed my swagger and laughed slyly.

I dropped his head in front of his body and told my mates that we need to dump his body. We had a decision to make and how we were going to get it off clean and then my associate told me that we need to dump the body on the outskirts of Baghdad in the middle of the night.

When we were preparing to wipe our hands clean so we wrapped his body in a blanket and we put his head in a backpack. We stopped on the highway and threw his body on the side. Americans all over the nation and the world got to see me slice somebody's head off and I got to kill somebody.

I didn't have any regrets because it was pissing me off that I couldn't come up with any evil thoughts. My thinking is that somebody else needs to get beheaded too.

Lucifer spoke to me and told me to get some more muthafuckers to behead. He wanted their souls and he told me that we needed to sneak over to Saudi Arabia and there I would find somebody else to behead. Then we got word that there was this guy named Paul and we saw it as an opportunity to make some American family feel tortured.

Ironically he was from New Jersey just like I was from before I got seduced by the darkside of the earth and wanted to cause wreak havoc and carnage throughout the land. When he was on a truck delivery we jumped him tied him up and took him hostage but this time we gave Bush an ultimatum.

We wanted them to meet our demands that we have some of the prisoners for Abu Gharib be released but Bush didn't want to see it that way. We gave Bush 72 hours to meet our demands and we already proved that we didn't give a fuck how he felt we wanted to see shit our way.

Again Bush wanted to show his nuts and he must've thought that we were bluffing and we gave him indication that we were serious by broadcasting it on Al-Jazeera network that we weren't playing. I think Bush failed to understand that when it comes to us that we're the bad guys and all bets are off.

That Friday came and the 72 hours and Bush still didn't want to hear what I had to say. Me and the boys decided that we were going to keep our end of the bargain and that was to behead him. So we decided to that it was time to show America what we were made of.

We snatched Paul up and we set up the camera and we were about to show him off and how we were going to kill him. That's when we fuckin' set up to the Al-Jazeera network on the internet and we waited until three o'clock U.S. Eastern standard time to show the horror.

We didn't want to be on television unlike the way it was when we killed Nick. Instead we put him face first on the floor and we put the knife to his throat and started slicing off his head and we could hear him scream and we grabbed a handful of his hair so we could get a grip on him while we cut his head off.

It only took 45 seconds to do the deed. We then dumped his body in an undisclosed location. Bush called our act barbaric. Hey I take personal pride in that and I thought of being a killer but not a barbarian because we're not in that age anymore.

We still weren't done then we kidnapped a handful of Turkish workers and a Korean soldier who was on a mission. We decided that America wasn't gonna be the only one to catch it that goes to anybody associated with the U.S. That's right they're straight catching it if we get our hands on one.

We gave the Korean government a deadline too to have them remove their associates and anybody that's in Iraq to get them the fuck out. Of course it had to be some shit so we ran it down in line. We made em' draw straws and the one that had the shortest straw was the one that was gonna get beheaded first and the second one would be the next to get it.

The one with the longest straw would live long enough to see the other two get beheaded. It ain't nothing new with all the chaos that's been going on in Iraq we hid the hostages in the spiderhole where they found Sadaam and the U.S. Troops are too stupid to know that's where we held them captive.

We took watches and turns and if they try to run you best believe that someone was getting killed. That Arab-American soldier for the U.S. Who claims that he was kidnapped that showed him being blindfolded at knife point was a fuckin' hoax and he tried to say that it was Al-Queda.

It says in the code of Jihad about killing another Arab but we don't see it like that. He just wanted to have something to do with us because he wanted to be put on discharge from the war that Bush lied about to get Saddaam and he was able to manipulate and brainwash the U.N. that Saddaam is evil and he funds us.

They couldn't find Osama and they couldn't find me so they go after the next best person and that's why he had to catch the brunt of the shit. We were about to behead someone else but he managed to escape. It was just a lapse in our watch and he got that off by getting away with his life. At least he can live to say that he wasn't going to be off with his head. I'm like being heartless and cold. I just want to try to come up with a new element of torture before I kill somebody. If it's your time to go then Lucifer gave me the green light to take you out of your misery. It's a war that I'm fighting and I'm trying to send a message that this is the way to go right now.

If we have to kill and take anybody allied with the U.S. we're straight taking hostages one by one. Bush is the one that thinks that sacrificing an American life is worth him being a stubborn bastard. He can stick by his guns and not do what we requested and we'll take it upon ourselves that any American isn't safe.

When we killed those Turkish drivers we just dump their bodies around the same area we dumped Nick. We wrapped their bodies in some plastic and threw their heads in a big ass duffle bag. We got that act of trying to annoy America out our system so we decided to cause some chaos in Europe.

We took our act over to London and we set some bombs on how we were gonna attack the British. We used some depressed Muslims that we thought had no will to live and we brainwashed them by telling them that Allah would be proud. It just had to use some powerful influence that they could do our dirty work.

So one Wednesday we went to London and we scoped out the prospects that we could use. We already crashed the planes into buildings we did that in the U.S. so we decided to take another route in letting the world that we were alive and kicking. When it comes to Al-Queda we play for keeps.

I was two wayed about the way I wanted it to go down. Then I contacted bin Laden and he approved the whole plan. I had his approval and that was all the support I needed. We wanted to catch a building off guard, the subway, one of those double decker buses.

We set them off in four different sections and we wanted to set them off during the London rush hour. We set them off between 8 and 9 o'clock am and we killed around forty people. There were about seven hundred people injured. We were a pretty disappointed because the casualty rate wasn't as high as we wanted.

Some muthafuckers did die and the rate went up. Now they got the tapes that showed our Al-Queda soldiers that had their backpack full of explosives. They can't charge them because they died in the honor of Allah. Don't they understand that the name Al-Queda's meaning is to sell.

We sell our acts of chaos to the world and we sell the evil that we want to inflict to those who threaten us and we're not afraid to bear our teeth. We ain't afraid to put shit out there that we start. We keep the Americans guessing what we're gonna do next.

The Americans like to know what we're up to. We make them keep the terror alert at elevated. We have the doubious distinction of havin the worst terror attack on American soil. When we get our hands on an American we're pretty much licking our chops thinking about it. It's like we love seeing their blood on our hands and wiping it with the American flag and to piss off Bush in the process.

Believe me we're the Al-Queda force and you can't have us played like a deck of cards that you may have us as the Middle East's Most Wanted because we don't get down like that. In order to get us you got to come and kill us because we're not afraid to die just like the American Hostages are when we were beheading them. You keep listening to Bush you're gonna write out a check that you can't cash.

"It's like round and round and round she goes where she stops nobody knows!"

Believe me we know when we will strike and how we want it to go down. We make the kill and strike before you don't even know it. We demand it that if you're not with us then there are heavy consequences and a price to pay for those who oppose us. Nobody is safe from us. Wjem you deal with Al-Queda just make sure you.....

"Sleep with one eye open!"

Death Warrant

(CHAPTER TEN)

Too many people I've made a career of slandering them when they call me out. They asked for Kahlil well they got me and it was more than they could chew. I have too many enemies that would love to make me look like a fool. There's too many weaknesses you showed me to know how to expose them and knowing how to handle you.

You haven't been to hell until I write up some of your weaknesses and break you down. You got my attention and you'll see who you pissed off and who's out to get you. That's right we're getting there and I want to show you that you don't have what it takes and you can tell your peoples to sleep with one eye open you pussy.

I just ripped all up into you and stripped you of all credibility. All they want to talk about is me and how you feel about the way you got dissed. When I'm out to finish you I won't quit until I smell blood. Even then it may not be over until I want it to be considered done.

Now you bought Dirty out of me and Kahlil can't help you all he sees is another enemy and that character just goes on you so bad that the name will be in your head when you get pissed. How many people do I need to shut up and I'm looking to hear you in silence. It's about time the world sees that I want to find another victim and see who dares to challenge me.

I've killed enough people in the books I wrote and I if you pissed off then I reached that point that it gets bigger than me speaking the words. It's come to me that the grim reaper has spoken to me. When I try to kill you I've been watching a lot of Law & Order to know how to cover it and not get caught.

Kahlil Weston

There's so many ways and the people I killed is just so ridiculous. I killed enough people chasing them naked with a chainsaw or bashing them in the head with a golfclub. I never get caught that I don't need to take it to trial and beat it like O.J.

Consider this a lesson that I'm trying to touch your soul compared to you getting under my skin and I will do it. I'll get out and at you. I want to get there and let's go until we can't breathe no more. Let's get to a point that the first one to lose his life didn't win.

I get scared but I know that my time will come when I got to go home to Lucifer and tell him how I had fun on the earth. Well not only am I gonna kill you on earth but you're gonna die when I see you in hell. Lucifer wrote up that death certificate and that you need to join us down there.

You must've really set me off if I'm saying that you signed your death warrant. It's like saying that your wanted for death and I need to touch you. Now who wants to see me chase somebody else naked with a chainsaw? Who wants to hear that Kahlil tried to kill somebody else? Who wants to be the next in line to say that the world's greatest writer is at it again?

That's right I'm going to hell and you're joining me. You never thought that I would be ready to say one more time that I got to pull you down with me. Tie you to a fuckin human size dart board while Lucifer and I throw pitchforks at you.

I'm itching to a point that I want to kill somebody.

"How would Kenyetta feel?"

Like I told Antoinette, I'll write a chapter about killing Kenyetta and do you think I fuckin' care? What do yo think I won't talk about my friends too. Well nobody is safe from me even when I go out and want to kill somebody. In this little soap opera there ain't no surprise about somebody coming back from the dead.

The animosity has grown to a point that it's not big enough for the two of us on the face of this earth and somebodys got to go. I seen this coming for some time that all bets are off and that something needs to be done. I got all this hatred and now it seems like that it's the only revenge I can taste. I'll be more satisfied when you're gone.

That's right you pretty much ask for death because that's what I'm thinking right now. Everybody already hates Wes and I see the kiss of death in your future. I'm in the mood for some pain. I mean some real intense pain. I know weaknesses on you and know how to attack you and I see it in your eyes. I smell blood all over you.

When I get that evil look in my eye all I can think about is going in for the kill. I see you as wounded prey. You think that you're really ready to get there but you're not. In order to finish me off you got to really see me dead to think that you got the better of me.

If you see it as that then it's winner takes all and the one who's dead is the one that isn't the winner. It's like the classic way of drawing. You draw first blood and I draw the final blow. It's only a matter of time before we meet again and I see you on my terms not when you want.

Even if we were best friends I see you as a deadly enemy. I got that hatred flowing for you. A side of me opened up that I never thought that never existed but it unlocked me. That side of me is like a side of me that you would hate to see. If you threaten me anyway that I feel like it could be the end of me you best believe that it's not gonna happen the way you envisioned.

All that tried and failed to take out the Wesman and they're forced to sit there and shut the fuck up because they realized that they didn't want to get there. They thought they were ready until I strip them of all credibility and left with them walking around with a tail in between their legs because they feel stupid and realize that it's not nice to fuck with me.

We have a turf war and it'll be the day before I ever want to smoke the peace pipe with you. I beat you once I don't feel like I have don't have nothing to prove because I pretty much showed that I want to quit while I'm ahead. Then you want to fight again and it already sticks out in your mind that I already got the better of you and it didn't sit to well with you that I got the last laugh and your smarting.

It burns in the back of your mind that the Wesman has outsmarted his enemy and that you don't like the fact that your ass got put out there and your left mumbling, stumbling, and fumbling yourself. Your saying.....

"That damn Weston!"

That's right that damn Weston did do it and you know I don't give a fuck if I did it and you will remember who I am when it's all said and done. I only opened up a few of your holes and I leave it like that. Then you have to find a way to get your revenge and you don't have a plan B because you didn't expect me to have a counter for your plan A.

I annoyed you so bad and got you so good, you even have to get back up and I don't think that's wise. I would advise against it because if you didn't learn the 1st time then what makes you think that you'll be successful the second time around? It's like playing chess and I have counters and I plan counters I have a plan A, B, or C.

In order not to have your warrant sent to you it's best to take the high road and do shit that will be used against you. I don't need a gun to shoot you because I shouldn't have to get my hands dirty because you think of me as an asshole. Well I feel this way this asshole just made you look like a bigger asshole then the asshole you called the asshole.

Your just mad because your ass got verbally kicked from this side of Voorhees to Camden. I must have this fire that just burns that it brings out a side of me that i never want to expose and it scares you and I like that. When I have you at my mercy I just want to bully you around. You thought that being a bully is something then get a load of me when I bully you worse.

I let you talk and talk and pick with me but if you don't know when to stop and you think O.K. I got him and before you know it. You bat an eyelash and it was just so fast it's like...

"Bang!"

You felt it and you know that I got the better of you and you're left in awe. First time araound that's a warning to leave me alone and that's to let you know now you're playing with fire. The second time then it's more serious then it was the first time. It's not much for me to do for the second time when you're trying to go for round two because of the devastation from round one.

It seems like that's what everyone is still talking about is what I fuckin' did in round one. That's all their talking about and it's like whatever you try to do will have very little impact and it has to upstage me and that's one thing in this lifetime that you'll never do is never steal my spotlight.

Once that happens and you know you can't win then you have to do the next best thing and that's seeing me dead. Maybe it's has gone a little too far and I don't back down from a challenge and I'm willing to give you a chance to redeem yourself.

O.K. It didn't work the first time and it backfired the second time then I guess there will be a third and fourth and fifth. It'll go on again and again until you finally get your one win. You already lost 50,011 other times and what makes you think you'll win now.

You're really that pissed off to a point that it has to be the way it is. I have a cool head but you push me over the edge. I got to be mean or I'm out of my nasty guy stage. When I'm at my nasty guy stage then you can see my side that I very rarely exposed.

There's this bullseye on both of our backs and we're both trying to hit that target. I already been accurate with the way I been hitting the yellow spot in the center and now you keep trying and you keep missing. Then it reaches a point that you got tired of trying or it's in your best bet that it's not wise to fuck with me and you already know that I'm not gonna lose.

I take it as a little thing at first but then I reach a point that I snap and it ain't what you bargained for. You might think you'll bump me from the spotlight but you really don't. Not as long as I'm around and my name is who it is you have no chance in hell in knocking me off and the bad news I'm still fuckin' breathing.

I was once told that revenge is better served cold and I wait to get back at you. I may tell you a date that when I'll strike. It's a joust that I'm involved in and it can be my worst nightmare coming true but I have to prove that I'm a warrior and that I can go against anybody that I'm matched up against and that I find a way to win.

You want to get at me and you made a little bit of noise to garner my attention and I hear you but I keep it within an earshot then you may get arms length and that's when I have to keep it close but when you look me eye to eye then it seems like I'm put on notice that someone new wants a shot at me.

So you want to take me on? You want me dead. This is how it can go and down. You finish me off and I'm killed and you think that you did the job but you didn't. It's something that grows inside and then it'll be another and another until you realize that your obsessed with taking out another enemy. Then you'll realize that it's become your life.

No matter what happens in my life I began to realize that I'll always have somebody out gunning for me and there's always gonna be a reason to be called out and I'm not gonna pussy out or back down. I have that look in me as a competittor that I have that male pride not to lose and if it takes a lot of me and I have to use all my energy to get that W then I will.

It may reach the point of no return and I know that I'll be left with a scar and I'm willing and ready to go to hell and I know that I'll survive. I already know when I'm in a battle and when I'm ready to face the world one more time then I know I have to be that one to go in the phone booth and put on my cape.

I have that quality and I have the secrets equipped to take you on. That's the difference between me and you and I can put on a front that makes me look like I can take it. You know it must be some shit if it made me go to a point that I have to start talking pretty recklessly and I'm doing it at a level that shows intelligance but I know that it's the way it has to go down.

Doing something for me was like you did sign your death warrant. It's not like you're gonna get off scott free and that'll be the end of it. That's only the beginning and it's at that time I never got a chance to say what I had to say and how it needs to be handled or addressed.

It was vintage Kahlil doing what he seems to do and that's beating another challenger and putting him at bay but they'll tell you that the way I did it was so masterful that it leaves you in awe about the way I did it. You have different ways to take on an opponent. I don't know what was going through that person's mind but it was like suicide by the way it happened and it makes you say....

"DAMN!"

I never claimed to be the choir boy. I don't know better and if it's in my blood to do some evil things. It doesn't have to even involve shooting it out with guns. We can get our knuckles bruised and we can keep going until one of us is pretty much close to permanently closing our eyes.

I'm pretty much always going in as the underdog. I like those odds because I'm not expected to win and I love to prove people wrong. It's this thing that comes out of me that makes me so resourceful that I'm facing these astronomical odds that I'm stepping into a hostile environment and a zone that I never been in.

It seems like my enemy thinks that I'll crumble and fold and that I'm scared to lose. I'm not scared to lose but I know I have to fight to survive that's the only way I'll win and if I go in with a defeated attitude then they'll see the weakness in my eyes.

I can't expose my weaknesses to you because I can't let you win and I look like the loser. I'm obsessed with winning like I am to jerseys and porn. To reach your goal you have to damn near kill me or leave me left for dead to acheive it.

It hasn't been proven that I've been sly about shit and how I roll in silence. I'm like a snake and I like to see you in pain. When I'm through with you I'll make you wish that you weren't born. I'll be the nightmare you'll never wake up from. Let it be written that when the death certificate is written that it ain't nothing new when it comes to messing with me in this day and age.

You'll wish you messed with someone else when it's all said and done. I got a lot to lose and I don't mind ruining my reputation and if it gets shot in the process I really don't give a fuck. I don't care how bad they tell me to stop and I don't care how much I cross the line you really pissed me off and I'm thinking about making you taste your blood and yeah I'm talking big shit about it.

You must really think that I must be that much of a loose cannon if I'm talking shit that way. Well I was pushed to the limit and it bought that streak that was unlocked and I been waiting to go off at any moment and that volcano fuckin' erupted and I have this green light to put it on you and I don't see that red light in me to stop.

You know that we were going to and that the state of mind we're in and I'm fuckin' you up and you'll realize that i have your number. You can put up a good fight for so long and you can just lick your wounds and if you want to go again. I'll be happy to oblige.

I'm playing chess with you and I see that checkmae in sight and you'll realize that you don't have nothing for Dirty. You'll fuckin' realize that Dirty is something real wicked. You wish you really had something for Dirty and then again once I beat you for the 50,011th time then you'll get it through your fuckin' head that you're not built for this.

Just a word of conscience is the fight worth you getting your reputation shot. Just know when to hold and how to fold. It's a whole different ballgame when you decide that you want to go against me. I want to be on your bad side after try to throw your weight around at me.

After it's all said and done it's back to basic. I just tune you out and just wait for the next one that wants to step up and be the next one to get a shot at Wesman. Believe me they never found Jimmy Hoffa and when I'm finished with you and I don't mind getting my hands dirty off your expense. When you came at me that's when you pretty much wrote your death warrant.

Ms. Wright
(SKIT)

Kahlil: I'm gonna miss you and Ryan around here Ms. Wright.

Ms. Wright: Well Kahlil it's time to move on and I met nice people but it's time to go.

Kahlil: Well yeah! I'll let you in on a little secret Ms. Wright! I thought you were kind of cute.

Ms. Wright (smiling): Thank you Kahlil!

Kahlil: You're not gonna hold this one against me are you?

Ms. Wright: No!

Kahlil: Ryan would kill me if he found out I said that shit!

Ms. Wright: Hmmm! Hmmmm! Hmmm!

Born a Pornocostal

(CHAPTER ELEVEN)

I know my fuckin' porn and I was baptized into the world of watching it. I been an advocate for porn back when I was nineteen and I'm thirty-one now it seems like I still don't get enough of it. They say I need a girlfroend well the porn is my girlfriend and at least I know it's there for me in those lonely nights.

I got so much porn that I said that I can give a way a tub full of porn and have much more to back on my computer and I make sure that's one habit that I'm proud to admit. I don't even pay rent but I have money to the porn.

I'm just addicted for the porn and you can say that I'm a pornaholic. I even got a job at the porn store and to me working in the porn store is like an alcoholic working in the liquor store. I'm notorious for porn and make no bones about the porn I have.

I'm a junkie for it and it's reached a point that I have so much porn I give it away if I don't look at the shit. I may look at the porn once maybe twice and a week after I have it's just old to me. I basically pick my porn by the actress and how many of them are on the DVD or the tape.

I still got my issues but that high of masturbation is like getting a hit of heroine. I have certain actresses that I watch and ask Ryan about me naming fifty porn stars off the top of the head in a five minute span and believe me he'll tell you.

Ask him about the time we went to his friend Blake's and Blake popped in a porn and I just looked at the back of Lana Sands' ass. I knew it from the bat and Ryan was left there in awe but he wasn't shocked that I knew who's ass that was.

If you talk about women in porn that I go crazy for I have to say that my favorite actress is Serenity. Serenity is built like a sister and she has that nice round ass, she's pretty and that's a bonus. It's like I see Serenity on the tape cover it's like I got to have it. Serenity is like the first round pick and it's mandatory.

I was a fan of Asia Carrera until I fell in love Serenity but I was gah gah with Asia Carrera. The thing with Asia is that I'm not that big on oriental women but she did it for me. She was more appealing to me when she got her body fixed up.

The porn must be my escape. I average about buying at least one porn tape a week. I once in a blue moon go real crazy in buying porn. I'll go off and just go on a porn shopping frenzy. I feel like porn is a healthy addiction. As long as you don't fuckin go and rape somebody and have myself in jail for some sort of sexual assault like Kobe was accused of.

I can't really say that I have a top ten but if I did the list would go like this. They would consist of...

1. Serenity
2. Asia Carrera
3. Kylie Ireland
4. Kendra Jade
5. Anna Malle
6. Stephanie Swift
7. Midori
8. Montana Gunn
9. Nici Sterling
10. Jasmine St. Claire

I have more porn than the average person. Those who say that they have more porn than me and I tell them that I fuckin' got about seventy DVD's and like sixty VHS cassettes and they say I got them beat. They come to me and wonder how do I stay with that much shit.

I get the criticism that I need a girlfriend and I shouldn't get that much porn. I know my history when it comes to porn and we can go actress to actress and I'll still be more equipped to know more than you. I get it poppin with so much porn that I'll start the champagne room somewhere else now like I did when I was at Kintock.

We were watching porn left and right in Kintock in Bridgeton. I made the champagne room and when Kahlil came through the door with the porn they knew what time it was. I wasn't the type of nigga to fuckin' have the porn sitting in my locker. You would see the tape once or twice and it was out my hands.

I was considered a hot corner and the staff knew about my bad habit of collecting porn. It's like Ron Jeremy dipped me in the water and not a pool of sperm and made me a religious man in my faith to porn. I just want to be ordained with watching hot women having sex and screaming out in satisfaction.

I wasn't really that big on Tera Patrick but she seems to be growing on me but I got to admit she likes she sucks a mean dick. I just got to ask how the hell can I sleep on her. I don't have any tapes on her except the one that has her giving out a blowjob. The tape is called jawbreakers. She seems like her jaw is unbreakable the way she be sucking that dick.

My mom has even took my porn and she's just jealous because I got more porn and I still can't get the habit kicked and it's been in my blood to collect just like you dialed 1-800.

Let me tell you something brother all my friends that talk to me will tell you I don't care who you are I'll talk about porn in front of anybody and be glad that I'm a junkie.

Since the days back before Jenna Jameson became the most famous porn star on the face of this earth that's when I became baptized in the porn. Now it seems like everybody wants to be like Jenna. Especially how Jenna Haze tries to be like her but she can't. Jenna has become so big that she has her own website called Club Jenna.

Jenna is like one of those realistic Barbie dolls. I bet a lot of people don't even know where she got the name Jenna Jameson. Sleep on this if you want but she's really Italian. Her real name is Jenna Massoli. She named herself Jameson after the Jameson drink.

I got the tapes on Jenna but any guy who's a porn collector has to have a Jenna Jameson tape. That's like equivalent to being back in the 80's that the average black man would have a Vanessa Del Rio in their stack. Now Jenna has gotten pretty corny because all she's doing is scenes with her husband. If it ain't her husband than she's doing a dike scene.

If I had to say even Mocha is looking good to me too. She has her twin sister Chocolate but for some odd reason Mocha is that chick that drives me wild. She has that pretty toffee skin. I got that battle of the black babes Midori vs. Mocha. She has those small little droopy titties but she has that real tight little body.

Then there's Lana Sands and she use to be my favorite porn star. Awww man! I didn't realize that Lana was white until I went to prison and I read an article on her. She said that she was half Thai and half Irish. The way Lana was sticking her ass in that Black Tail and saying that all her lovers were black was pretty mind blowing.

When I was eighteen I use to be sold on Janet Jacme that ass was so big that it looked ridiculous. Her and Serena Williams' ass is running neck and neck. I only have one tape with Janet now and when I had my collection I might've had around I say fifteen to twenty.

The thing I liked about Janet was that she fuckin' doesn't get it on with girls and she's straight. You could just have her lay flat on her stomach and leave a drink on her ass because that's how firm and right that thing was looking. It's like you could be a bartender and serve the drinkers at the bar. I don't buy that many tapes on her now.

I guess because of the time going by so fast and her being a porn star in the late eighties and early nineties it's just outdated to me. I keep saying that I need to buy a tape on her more often but I don't. I don't know because I see a different tape and I just lose track that it's there.

When I caught this bad habit of looking at porn I was a teenager but it got out of control in the last several years. My addiction to porn is like Tracy's is to beer. When I use to work at Labor Ready last year I fuckin' use to go next door to the porn store and buy a DVD and take it back with me to the homeless shelter.

Then I got caught with having porn in my locker and they made me get rid of it and if I didn't I was gonna get discharged. I remember how I had to drag a laundry bag full of tapes down Atlantic Avenue and then having to catch two buses out to Lindenwold to get to my man Tony's and having to leave the shit with him until I got my own place.

The day I moved out that shelter and went to Hi-Nella I came back for my porn. It's the only thing I know and you know it would only be so long that I be away from my toys. When you step in my apartment you'll see all sorts of porn scattered on the floor.

My aunt won't even step in that bedroom and people that walk through the door and are saying.....

"Goddamn boy you got all that porn!"

That's right it's my motherfuckin place and when you step in my closet you see the images that I downloaded off the internet and printed out and taped them to the wall. I call that masterpiece "Keeping it in the closet". Ryan's nigga Kareem knew about Serenity and I was surprised that he knew a few of those porn stars. It's too bad that his porn I.Q. isn't update with mine.

I think of porn as a form of art of women that want to express themselves to help some of these men control their desires that they want to have sex with. My mom told me once that she knew I was having sex and she knew it was with myself.

I even feel like I corrupted my mom too. The porn she watches is the porn she got from me. It's like if I look at the porn once whether it's VHS or DVD it's considered old to me and I may or may not look at it again. My porn is like me having a handful of underground mixtapes that haven't been released.

There's just so much porn for me to buy that I still can't enough of it and it's my drug of choice and I must admit that porn to me is like reciting the twelve step program when an alcoholic admits that they're powerless over their addiction and that there is a higher power.

Fuck that I don't see it that way. I talked about giving up porn and going into be saved at thirty-five and now I don't know if I'm a man of my word. The porns got me flippinng that when I think that I bought enough porn it just ain't good enough.

My mom jumps on me about the porn that I buy and that it's not healthy. I find it healthy if you can't have sex with a girl just have sex with yourself. Wrap some toilet paper or a paper towel around your penis and pop some porn and just imagine who's the actress you want to fuck.

You see how technology is nowadays with how the porn industry is. It's a billion dollar a year industry and just the money that's fed into it is so surreal. Like with the DVDs they have that virtual sex shit with some of your favorite actresses and you could imagine yourself having sex with them.

I bought one of those DVDs and I have to say that I'm pretty impressed the way they have it set. I bought this Stacey Valentine DVD called "Chasing Stacey" you get to comand where you want her on the DVD and it was something I never seen before.

I do be chasing and it seems like when it's all said and jest I srill won't have enough porn in my lifetime and don't plan on quitting on the habit. I'm married to the porn like I never been before and it's my most greatest addiction and I love it.

A guy can't live without a girl alone if he ain't getting laid. At least I can be open and honest about me when it comes to watching porn. I remember when Jeniece Armstrong wrote a fuckin article in the Philadelphia Daily News about how men were always shopping for porn and that there are very few women that even look at that shit.

When Jeniece said that I called her up right away....

(I know Jeniece she works with my mom and they're best friends at the Daily News)

I told her that she would surprised that there are more women out there that watch porn than she realize. When I had a talk with her about it she seemed like she was in the conversation. I told Jeniece that the next time she writes an article about that make sure she comes to me for some info because my IQ when it comes to porn is to the ceiling. She agreed to take me up on it.

What Jeniece fails to realized is that women know some of those actresses they just don't tell you. You would be surprised with the names they know and you would've never pictured it. I see them and they'll sit there and watch it with you too. Girls get turned on looking at that shit.

When Tracy and I use to collect porn we use to swap them like baseball cards. The thing is that Dominic would fuckin' freeload off Tracy for porn and the thing is that Dominic would never bring the shit back. Dom makes more money than Tracy and I or Aaron for that matter and he has to get free porn from us.

I can't say I blame Dominic for being such a goddamn freeloader because Tracy was stupid enough to let him do it. If it was me in Dom's shoes I don't think I would freeload off them. Certain actresses turn me on and I watch a different kind of porn from what they watch.

Trace can watch the black porn and Aaron or Dom for that matter. I was into that white porn and not that it bothered me because I felt like they were more creative and my taste in watching porn is far more different. Like I'm into that upperclass porn.

I can look at the Jenna Jamesons, the Stephanie Swifts, the Serenities, the Lana Sands, the Kylie Irelands, the Asia Carreras, and they'll look at the Obsessions, the Mochas, the Chocolates, the Menaja Trois, the Kittens, the Jordan McKnights and the list can go on.

Honestly I just like white porn better because it's more creative and I guess because I been so white girl crazy since Shay that it's just my preference. Porn is like an escape for me and it helps me. It helps your imagination run wild about some type of girl you desire. You may like em' skinny, you may like them thick, hell you may like em' fat, or you might like them grandmother old.

I like to keep them young. I think the only woman I think I can see in porn that's pushing fifty is probably Ona Zee and Nina Hartley. Well Ona Zee is about fifty two years old and she did it for me back when I was about sixteen. I thought she had the best body in porn when I was about seventeen.

Then that brings us to Nina Hartley who's about 47 or 48 and she has a really nice body and still doing it in the porn biz. Well should I say an excellent body especially for pushing fifty. I guess because I'm moreof a legs person and she has really nice legs that it's a turn on and the fuckin' fun part is she'll fuck a black person too.

I thought that her lower part of her body was tight and that Ashlyn Gere was the only other one that could've touched Nina's lower body. Nina looks better from head to toe eversince she got her boob job. It's just that any guy in the porn game or buys porn knows who she is. If I have the money and it's very rare you can buy porn on Nina in the store but if I run across it I make sure I take advantage of it.

Another girl who I like from head to toe is Kylie Ireland and the body that she has is like she's fuckin healthy as a horse. When she got her head turned red she's even looking sexier than she was before. I guess whenever I see a Kylie Ireland video that I'm feenin' to have that in my collection. Surprisingly some women know who she is they just won't tell you about it. She doesn't get the attention that Jenna Jameson gets.

I mean she's tight and I remember when Tracy put me on to her and that's when I became big on her.

I bought this video called "Face Jam" but I really bought the video becaseu ti ahd Stephanie Swift and Nici Sterling on it and when Tracy told me about Kylie Ireland I looked at it as a bonus I knew about her for a while but he put me on to her when I was buying porn from the halfway house and sending it to him.

That's when I became big on her. I was into that shit but than when I was all into being so fascinated into Serenity that it's like she takes control of all the porn I buy. I would go to a porn convention just to meet some of those chicks and take pictures of them. I know that it's my dream before I die in this lifetime that I go to a convention.

There's still not enough porn and it'll never be enough and when I have porn that I don't like that's cluttering up space. I'll just fuckin' give it away that's the type of person that I am. I just give to the needy. Those who need to get their little collection up a little. I'm carrying the big guns. When it comes to me and my porn I say...

"Amen to that!"

Chess Ain't Checkers

(Chapter Twelve)

Keep your friend close but your enemies closer. Understand that when you have an enemy they're your opponent. You study your opponent and find out their weaknesses and turn them into a strength. That's what makes me a name to stay away from. At times it's good that I'm locked in a feud it brings out that cerebral side of me.

I'm not gonna lie my life would be so boring if I didn't have any enemies. You couldn't imagine the rush I feel locking in combat with them. I have enemies like you couldn't even imagine. My friends could be my enemies. Close at one point and now it's nasty to a point that it ain't over until my last word is said.

If my last word was so damning there's no need to dignify it with a response. I can take the high road and say fuck it. I did what I had to do. In a way keeping your enemies closer in a way is fun. You want to keep up with them like you're keeping up with the Joneses. The problem is that the enemy has been keeping tabs on you and you have to be aware.

In another battle am I? It seems that way. Like a Jedi Knight I'm swinging a lightsabre against someone and you best believe that it's either yin or yang. Am I fighting for the rebellion or am I breathing heavy and pledging my allegiance to the dark side. I guess since my mind can be filled with revenge that I'm seduced by the dark side of the force.

I couldn't tell you how powerful I feel when I can write what the fuck I want. It's like I'm in that shoot to kill mentality. All this shit is premeditated when I'm out to hunt down the opposition. Kill now no questions need to be answered after the massacre occurred. However it needs to be handled if the messenger needs to be killed than so be it.

I concede nothing. If I have white I'm on the attack if I have to play with black I'm still in attack mode. When I get into that writer's mode I get into that focus mode. A total concentration has to take place when I write these chapters. Best believe that I want to win in anything.

Nobody likes to lose. At times you have to lose. Fighters have to lose and at times you have to pick and choose your battles. Maybe the competitor in me likes the challenge. Being challenged lets you know that your opponent wants to best you. You may run across someone that is just your superior and now your competitive mentality has to go to another level. They saw your right and now you have to be ambidextrous to get them to counter.

I keep my weapons hidden and bring them out only if needed. Like a mad scientist who shows you one thing but has something better than the product he's showing the world. Just when they think they caught up with you then you bring out something else to have them thinking because you upgraded. Now they're scurrying to keep hanging with you.

When I get to use my weapons they're like toys that I been itching to play with. I been waiting to unleash hell with the weapons I been holding back. It makes my weapons impressive when you wish you could have the shit I have in my possession. They have that fascination the way you're displaying it.

To let my opposition know that I have no weaknesses, I hope you read my wikipedia to see what you can use against me. Thinking you can take your little cheap shot and walk away unscathed is so too vanilla for me. Like you did it and chuckled. It doesn't work like that for me.

Since you can do it then you need the flairs for the dramatics. When I study opponents best believe I'm finding the advantage to keep you on the defensive. I'm like a tennis returner who's out to break your serve. Depending on how far the match goes and the measure of intensity that had to go into this lets me know there's a rivalry and now you met your competitor.

Your rival will never concede to you. At the same time he's never gonna believe that you're better than them. It gets fiery and there's nastiness involved. It can turn out to be a blood bath and the next time you meet you know that you got to bring it and your "C" game ain't good enough. From the door you better be on your p's and q's.

Never tell your opponent your secrets on how you take them on. Let them figure it out. If they find out your scheme and start whooping your ass then you know that you need to lick your wounds and come up with a new strategy. If they start talking shit and saying what they know what you're doing then they have you figured out and none of your tricks work. To them you've become predictable.

In a rivalry and you faced that opponent so many times they know you as well as you know them. At times they'll steal your secrets and use it to their advantage. It goes on from generation to generation everybody has a particular situation where they want to beat you. Even the outsiders that you don't have a rivalry with are also out to beat you.

Every opponent has different ways you have to combat them. Some matchups work well with other. You may have one opponent figured out but not the other one. Then the opponent you're beating can beat an opponent you can't beat but you can't beat the opponent that you're beating. That's just the laws of science.

I have a rival in chess. Well I had many rivalries in chess. I played against super chess player and then there's the less than super. I have played people that I was better than and now there are some who studied the ways and are able to topple me. My main rival in chess is my nigga Kendall Miller.

I met him when I was in Ancora he was a staff member and I was supposedly the unstable patient. When I was in the Holly Ward there I was crushing opponents on my tier. Then they wanted to match me up against the supposed best in the ward a dude by the name of Dewitt Crandell. He claimed that he didn't want to play me because he knew he could beat me. I don't see it that way.

I even told him lets get the board and prove to me that you could beat me. He backed down from my challenge. If he's better than me prove it to me. I declared myself the best by default. Nobody even tried to face Crandell they came down for me. I had staff members stepping off their wards to come and face me.

I can't lie I was pretty flattered that they wanted a piece of me. They wanted to get at me. I was the nigga running around with the belt around my waist and somebody else wanted what I had. What I got is what they want. While I was in there defending that chess title I stayed as hungry as them. I treated it as if I was the challenger and they were the champions. I had to use that reverse psychology and pretend that I'm the hunter.

The thing about the challenger is that there more dangerous without the title. They're hungry and it's a feather in their cap if they can knock off the champion. If I lose that one little chess game I take it as you're not gonna go 82-0 in the NBA. No matter how good I am you're not gonna win every game.

In my eye I considered myself the best in chess until you beat me frequently. I'm not talking about one day you beat me two out of three do it four times a week by week and I'll feel different. I feel like this you're trying to catch me and if I'm the champ I'm defending the title. You have to beat the champ the champ doesn't have to beat you.

I believed that title belongs to me because I paid my dues and worked my way through the ranks to get it. That's how it needs to be done. It's done by beating your opponent and to a point that it garnered the attention to let it be known that I'm real and I coming hard. You hear these challengers want that want to take you on and they haven't paid there dues. You might have garnered my attention from a bird's eye view but when you go against me it's a different ballgame.

When you study the opponent you find their flaws and when they think they're untouchable you bring it to light. It'll make them think about it but they act like it didn't bother them. Oh it did they can act tough as nails but I got their attention.

My enemies and my opponents need to understand that I have no weaknesses. Not even kryptonite can touch me. I'm not gonna tell you so you can know what to do against me. You got to find it I'm not gonna tell you. I'm not that stupid to just tell you how to beat me.

My thing is this I don't come at you unless it warrants it. It's not like you're innocent and you best believe until you hear a Kahlil response. I fuckin' love trumping' people. They can cry and whine until the cows come home about what I did and I can care less. Save the drama for Osama did you forget to tell people about the shady acts you did to warrant a response.

Lucifer must be transmitting messages to me in tongues or something when I come up with these ideas. They can be twisted but revenge can be served cold. No matter when I serve it to you best believe that it's gonna be served hot. I can dish it at any temperatures. It's like strike first ask question later.

Chess is a mental game. The decisions you make on the board is the decisions you make in life. I never realized the challenges no how to play chess until I learned how to play my freshman year at Camden High. Losing a game of checkers don't mean shit to me now. Checkers is pissy compared to chess.

You have a chess board in place and you set up your pieces and now the riddle to solve is how to attack your opponent. He knows what you're gonna do and he anticipates it then you have to come up with second to third options because he knows your first. Steal his pieces off the board and cripple his defenses. Get the queen off the board and you have them at a total disadvantage. Take all his pieces off the board leave only the king and leave that opponent naked on the board.

You see those superhero movies and what's the excitement about the hero. He finds a way to win despite all odds stacked against him. Heroes use their brains and you know they have to find a weakness on that enemy. It's all about the matchups, how do you measure up against your opponent. When you continuously keep going at it with the same opponent after a while it gets boring.

That's why the movies are better. The enemy has there plots and how to beat the hero and it's the heroes job to defend not only himself but to all those who are dependant on him or her to keep the world safe. You get chills down your spine because this ain't one of those cupcake game of bingo. I tell you this now I fuckin' hate to play checkers but chess....

"Ahhhh! That's the challenge!"

The object of the game is checkmate. Chess is played in many competitions just like The U.S. Senate lobby behind the scenes to pass or not pass bills. Enemies come and multiply in many directions. Some come out of nowhere or they're underneath your nose and you never detected them. They tend to pounce on you when you're in a vulnerable position.

The problem is they think I'm just a check on the board and all they got to do is jump me or blow me for not taking the jump. The thing is for me is that once I learned how to play chess I hate playing checkers. To be honest checkers stink, it's not challenging.

When I write books and especially when I'm out to crush my enemies you have to understand that I have the home field advantage. Usually my track record proves that I have that aura of invincibility. I can go on the road and win there but there's so much joy winning on the road. In the book all I got to do is hold serve.

In my eyes a feud with me doesn't start until I issue a full throttled assault to insult you. You can respond and best believe the minute your back is turned I have a response faster than lightning. It happened so fast that you can't prove that I did it. While you think you were watching me I was watching you watching me.

I can find out where you live and I can do some graffiti when you wake up. It's like you made me take it there and trump you up. Believe me I did my homework when I attack. I wanted to dish it hot but cold was the way to go.

My enemies can be sneaky and they come out of leftfield. They work behind the scenes and are hypocrites. They already had a low opinion of you but they kept it to themselves. They sit back when you're down and take their shots when you're in a vulnerable state. They get their little cheap shots in then try to tuck their tail in between their legs and act like they don't know shit.

Those type of enemies are like pitbulls when they attack. They act all normal but they lock on a target and fuck shit up. Then when animal control gets them and they know they're about to be put to sleep they're all innocent. It was all fun and games but when they have to suffer the consequences then comes them beg for mercy thing.

When you're a teen you don't know shit. In your twenties your still pretty stupid hit your thirties and you think more clear. I feel like the thinking woman's sex symbol I didn't feel that way since I turned 30. I have so many ways to come after you and I'll use any tactic I can to get the job done. I got counters for your responses. I have more than a plan A up my sleeve.

However the job has to be done it's gonna be done. It's for me to know and for you to find out. It's better to keep you off balance and have you wondering what's gonna happen next. You heard how helter skelter works. It means you don't know what's going to happen. If you want to test me and take me up on my challenge than you dare to challenge me.

Wow! I give you credit for thinking that you can take me on. Kind of suicidal but you're in an everything to gain and nothing to lose situation. I love shitting on people and they have no way to counter my response. They wanna cry what I did but fuck what they did to trigger the beef. All that got lost up in the response. They're just mad because my response trumped theirs.

Understanding this when it comes to dissing and talking shit you got bring you're "A" game. I wouldn't see it no other way. Bringing out your "C" game is pretty feeble and that leaves you vulnerable to being hurt. I'm out for revenge and I want to see you at my mercy. I'm smelling blood like a wolverine can smell a dead meal.

Understand if you play checkers with me is like a cheap thrill game. It's like if a six year old beats me in Mortal Kombat. It doesn't mean shit. I'm into playing that long hard fought game you put your thinking cap on just play chess. I'm into mind games and trying to find away to beat my opponent.

I'm locked in competitor's mode and trying to gain the advantage. Always staying steps ahead of my enemies while they're checking me always trump ahead of your opponent. Never let em' know what you're thinking and if you do just have your plan B if plan A doesn't go as expected.

In the game of life every stage is a chess match. Understand that when you sit down and stare that opponent in your eye always remember that the object is to get the person in checkmate. I don't give a fuck how many pieces you have off the board you can still get beat. Everytime I write this shit and I show it off to the public I'm already playing roulette.

I'm flipping that coin like Harvey Two-Face and I know if it lands on the side that's fucked up it could be the end. I don't think anybody is counted out until the day you're pushing daisies. I couldn't tell you how many times I've been counted out and time and time again I keep making news. I take calculated risk, it may backfire but that's the risk I take.

You don't think that when you're hollering at a girl that they're already playing chess with you. Like they don't study you to see where you're at. I think the hard part is getting past first base. Better yet every base you try to get to is a chess match especially when you're sliding into home. Women are more mental while guys are more physical. You got to let em know where you stand. I have a better grip on them now than I once did.

The mentality I carry has to be sharp and witty. It can be sneaky and tactical just when you think I let something go you may got done dirty. It's all about strategy and how you plan it. You got people out there that might be copying your style and running with it. They're on some biting shit and they like your style because they can't come up with one of their own.

Even if I get older you think I lost a step. If I did I'm gonna work extra harder to let you know that I didn't to get that step. I carry that kill and crush you mentality. If you show that weakness it's definitely gonna get exposed and I have no plans on letting up. If you don't want me to rub it in then stop me. It's not the 21 point rule in Madden where the games automatically over. Really understand that I'm not out to just win I'm out to blow you out.

Writing My Indictment

(Chapter Thirteen)

If it has to go down that way then it's gonna happen. I consider this a dare to see if I'll crack. The threats and the rumors that I hear will never ever stop me. They feel like me possibly falling in love with porn will be my downfall. I use all that heat to fuel my fire and raise another topic on my resume.

This is a dare I assume to say Wes you need to stop what you're doing. Now murderers wanna say...

"I'll read about you in the Courier Post!"

Yeah! You will but it won't be for murder. I feel like if I said it then I will not break. I will not turn and will say what I feel. I took the secret oath as an author to tell y'all to kiss my ass if you don't like the shit I say.

As I just written what I speak they say I go too far. Put me under review so the D.A. can file a felony on me supposedly. I tell you what...tell them that Wes was the nigga that wrote the shit. What's another rumor gonna do to me now. Rumors don't have me breaking out in any sweats.

Pressure? What pressure? My pipes don't bust lets make that clear. This is my show and I'll write it my way. I wrote this shit and I'll say what I like. If I choose to talk about killing people to being a verbal nymphomaniac then that's my damn choice. You really think me going off is gonna put me at halt?

"It's my shit! I said it and try and stop me!"

I just began to learn how to swing my nuts with pride. I write what makes my shit interesting and I'll push buttons at will. You got child molesters running free and sickos worse than me. Instead of putting me under review worry about the fucks that could be molesting your kid.

Before I came along the world was already fucked up with issues. I just write it I didn't do it. The world will still have issues when I'm dead and gone. I say shit obviously to get your attention just to see how much I have shock value. Since you think I'm crazy then I have an impulse to do something else crazy. Now I wanna say more crazy shit to sell books.

Remember I'm the lovesick puppy who even gets in trouble for liking girls. I just expressed my feeling for crying out loud. I should've realized I put myself at risk when I opened up my feelings. I did what I had to do. I was a little nervous but hey that's how a gunslinger lives and that's on the edge.

There's a number of fucks who think that I lost my fuckin' mind. The more I receive criticism the more I think my book is ready to take center stage. Fuck the police threats that I get they're not gonna do me in. They can chew a fuck cocks for dialing 911 and be faggots for being hurt over some fuckin words. I just keep it in my formula of tricks.

The police and the prosecutor won't make me collapse. They definitely won't intimidate me to take the shit out that I wrote. What I say stands. I say what I feel and I won't back down from my comments. If you don't like the comments that I use then I guess that's tough shit. The police wasn't threatening me then and if you call them I'm gonna kill you.

What the fuck are you gonna have me charged with assault with a deadly pen? Writing alleged threats for my coronation to allegedly being indicted. I'll have the grand jury left in a hung. All you need to know is that they'll be fans of mine when it's all said and done. I dare any cop to cuff me if they try to tell me how to run my book.

"And you muthafuckers still don't get it do you?"

If I wrote chapter that are medium then I need to raise the level of it being crazy. It's in my blood to speak it. You can't stop me the only thing you can hope to do is contain me...

"They say that shit on ESPN!"

I'm no t the least bit worried about me being in trouble for my work and it's in writing. Been there, done it lived it, went through it. I know what putting shit in writing can do. I got to be smart about it and use my words selectively.

I won't back down because I say what I feel about shit around me. I feed off my emotions that's what drives me. It drives grown ups to a point that they think that I need to be put behind bars. They feel like I need to take the rap and I'm not allowed to fire back. I'm suppose to sit there and fuckin' take it.

Muthafuckers tell me to show a little compassion and think about what you're doing when you say it. Now since its written, I spoke it, now you already read it. What new twist will my fate put me in? It'll put me in new shit again. Now I know what I can write because my shit is already under the microscope.

Tell a girl I want to be friends like I wrote it back in 1994. She wants to take the story and run with it. Blew it up like she was a victim under attack. Used my own words and twisted them up like I tried to hurt her. Fuck that shit now the only category I see her as is a....

"B-I-T-C-H!"

I think it's pretty ridiculous to blame me when I'm being singled out. Wes is allegedly under arrest for supposedly speaking it. They want to confiscate my shit and put it under police review. I'm just ready to burn in the hotseat for talking greasy. Just to showboat my fuckin' personality.

"I gave Hollie Tucci a chance to turn me over to the police and I knew she wouldn't do it!"

I'm being real arrogant when I say it too. You fuckin' dummies should've realized that when I put the shit in her hands. I was just smart enough to say it and get away with it. I only did it to test her and I damn sure didn't do it out of love.

This is an open dare to anybody who says that I really lost it. The ones that couldn't stand me, I already dropped a battery down your gas tank. The minute you start your car, you're blowing up to smithereens and you silly muthafuckers will be paranoid the minute you put your key in the ignition.

I already know amongst my readers I'm the meanest and the baddest. When it comes to my books the only nigga that sets the rules is me. Y'all can't be serious to think it's evident that this will be used as evidence against me. I have the right to remain violent anything I say and do will be held against you.

Me going to jail over writing books? I presume that the assumption will land me some sort of conviction. I ain't worried about it. I want to go prison again anyway and I'll get minimum status when I go to CRAF. I'll max out from the halfway house like I did in 2000.

I'm not really in the mood to be all smiles. I'll say what I feel and won't give a damn about it. Put me in that position and I'll come out swinging. Use a selective set of words of choice at my disposal like it ain't shit.

Is the evidence stacked against me to have me convicted yet? Reasons to have the Wesman locked the fuck up. Like I'm scared shitless. Hearing that I'm going to jail for what I wrote speech has gotten pretty tiresome; personally it pisses me off. I might talk about someone and muthafuckers will get it confused that it's them. I want to say...

"Where the fuck are you getting your information?"

Get the fuck outta here! They don't tell what I can and can't say. It's my fuckin' mouth and I'll say what I want. I didn't make any body read me. I do this shit my way. The more controversy the more marketing. I'll use this as leverage to make it better.

Take away my pens and I may be more tempted to buy swords. Just to mix up my words I might switch my language to speaking in tongues. That way it saves me bail money. It's already some bitch named Tanya Menton is so stupid that she has white-out confused for anthrax.

All this hype about me being singled out is a way for me to insult your intelligence. Don't get mad because I had the testicles to say it and I was only making up a fictional chapter. You muthafuckers need to go twitch somewhere else.

The first time I make my shit public and look who was out to get me. Left heads totally fucked up. Left people laughing. I had you believing that I had screws loose….

Troy: The whole kitten caboodle!

Now to make my book really look bad I get awarded wit police threats and niggas that can't stand me were reading me faithfully. Now that's contradiction for saying you hate Wes. All you need to do is add fuel to the fire and see how much hell I raise.

Words? Goddamn! Words hurt? I know they do. That's why they tried to lock my black ass up in the first place. Have me locked up and have them throw away the key. If you really lock for this shit then I know that the Camden County Justice System is that twisted. I know that their system is already retarded. I'm a goddamn taxpayer I got first amendment rights. I refuse to be censored.

Now if you flash those teeth that doesn't mean I'll yield. I always got the green light to write at will. If I got the ammunition I'll damn sure fire the gun. All I hear is a bunch of barking but no biting. At least when I bite I make it look pathetically obvious.

Let's see what other chapters can I write to get Dirty indicted…

- ☐ Writing about how I killed Chandra Levy.
- ☐ Abducting the body of JonBenet Ramsey.
- ☐ Shooting people with a trench coat on.
- ☐ Tying some gay guy to a post and beat him until he wishes he was dead.

Chalk up another set of felonies for me. I have no limits to the mayhem I cause. It goes from Tracy Clark to Troy Riggs but it gets dumped on that S.O.B named Wes Daddy Mack. I look at it this way I ain't got nothing to lose from writing this shit. I'll strip you.

My reputation is already shot. I can't look anymore of an idiot that I already look in your eye. Hey…I've been called worse shit than that. Being the poster boy just makes me look like a scapegoat. I feel like giving these muthafuckers a raspberry every time they say "Wes is going to jail!" It ain't gonna go down like that.

When I fall it won't be until my tombstone is etched in marble. If I collapse I'd rather do it in Hollie Tucci's eyes. If I go down I'm not tapping without a fight. If Wes is defeated then he's taking a few names down with him. That's the way I'm gonna let it go down.

I can't see it happening. Wes being arrested because my shit is hotter than a Donald Goines novel. Now I damn sure know you underestimated who I am. I was intelligent enough to speak it and you're stupid and blind enough to throw up the prejudice eye.

They want to accuse me of being guilty of the following acts and it goes like this…

Stalking Hollie Tucci?

It's fabricated she's not gonna file charges.

Stalking Guerdy Baguidy?

She doesn't even have a fuckin' case and I thought they threw those charges out.

Talking about 9/11?

You wish.

Liking Antoinette Ragone?

Antoinette: You know what Kahlil!

Dirty bin Laden?

Heh! Heh! Heh!

Basically y'all need to stop pissing me off or I'll respond. A letter of warning and I mean….

"No way!"

…you'll ever stop the Wes Daddy Mack. Confiscate my pens to prove that I'm considered a lost soul. I already proved on too many occasions that pen can be mightier than the sword.

In Kahlil We Trust

(CHAPTER FOURTEEN)

"I would look good on a dollar wouldn't I?"

We're going green this chapter. What's this shit about don't listen to a word Kahlil says? People really fuck me up!

☐ Don't listen to anything he says.

☐ Don't trust him!

☐ Stay away from him!

The beauty about writing when I write is that it's all about me. A part of my formula is that I try to keep it real in some of the things I write. I write chapters when I go crazy but at the same time if you're going to speak the truth at times, don't be afraid to make fun of yourself. You get respect from your peers when you keep it real to your viewers.

I now understand I'm still public enemy number one in a lot of eyes. Next thing you know I'll be a pissed off black man with a Muslim name who plots bombings with Bill Ayers.

Still today the mystery of why I was in Ancora. I have no idea what possessed Yvonne to have me sent and she's the one that started this whole thing. People try to act like parents are always right and they're not. The bible says in the commandment to honor thy mother and father well I have trouble with that now. My father's dead now and the situation with Yvonne is fucked up to the point of no return.

This fuckin' woman wants me evaluated and wonders why I'm so screwed up and I wonder where I got it from. I began to realize things about her that I never saw because I was totally blinded. I bet people thought when I went to Ancora that I was walking around with a straight jacket on. I could imagine the rumors that were started.

The reason I went to Ancora was because Yvonne wants to play the tired ass restraining order act the minute I get out of jail and she wants to shoot off her jibs. Then she wants to hide behind the cops and I kept getting sucked in. After that latest act with the restraining order and somebody keeps beating you with the same tired act I had to learn that you have to change your gameplan. I did that the problem is that Yvonne didn't.

I gave probation Yvonne's address when I was in jail back in 2002. When I was sentenced while I was still serving out the 364 day jail term I was approved for the address. The same day I get out of jail like I wrote in "The Young and the Wesless" the "Four hours of Freedom" chapter she gets me arrested before I even made it home. I talked to Jenice that day and you would think you're glad to see someone and your present is a trip right back to jail.

Anyway to fast forward when she got me arrested for a third time off the restraining order act for the third time back in 2003, I was only guilty of a punk ass criminal trespass and that asshole judge Natal had the nerve to write me up for violation of probation and has me held for six months over her fuckin' ass.

I told this other dipstick public defender Patrick Malloy about Yvonne lets me use the address for probation but starts playing the restraining order card the minute I get out of jail. He then puts two and two together and the Camden courts had the nerve to fuckin' postpone my court date for two months and when I went back two months later they postponed it for another month talking this bullshit about that I needed to be psychiatrically evaluated. That's why I went to Ancora.

Then I'm kicked while I'm down. Soon as your enemies hear about your misfortune they want to take advantage of you at your weakest point. Now I had an enemy stab me like Brutus did Caesar and it made me say et tu.

You would think that after Phase One shut down I could finally have a peace of mind. I'm still going to give you a piece of my mind and whether or not you like it I'm still gonna explain it like this. I didn't have a problem putting Cucu-CUNT-o on notice.

I thought six years removed from verbally kicking Sonja's ass that I would shut her mouth in 2004. After I dog shitted on her lawn she wants to act like she didn't do shit. She did a plenty when my black ass was sitting in Ancora.

She was calling Ancora telling them the 411 about me telling those assholes I was trying to kill people. I like to bomb shit had me answering questions to the staff about the dirt on me. Not only did she do it once but twice. Like I once said….

"First time shame on you second time shame on me!"

What the head scratcher to me was I thought we were close. I will admit I was totally taken off guard on how she went behind my back. When I confronted her about the situation I gave her a chance to address it and she didn't I was too gullible to realize deep down that she did.

I'd rather have Yvonne get me arrested off a restraining order than be stabbed in the back.

"…and that bitch did do that!"

What pissed me off more was that she wasn't adult enough to say she was wrong. She had the nerve to play like she was the vulnerable victim. Like I came out and attacked her and started this fuckin' feud. I didn't do shit to her to warrant a cold shoulder. If she didn't want to be friends anymore I'd rather her tell me.

What I thought was a real fuckin' joke is how she had the nerve to call Antionette about what I did to her.

"Like she expected something to be accomplished!"

All it did was flatter me to let me know that I made her jump. When Antionette told me that I was pretty flattered that Sonja was pissed. Somebody had to put the bitch in her place. I wasn't in the mood to play Mr. Nice Guy. I was out for blood and she thought that was gonna be the one to put the nail in the coffin. Like Pink said…

"I Ain't Dead Yet!"

I still have tricks in my sleeve. In a way I still don't understand when was this her fight. From what I remember I wasn't feuding with her. My feud was with a fat bitch named Lentz and a horny child molester named Valentine.

I said it once I'll say it for the 50,011th time that they drew my ire when they got me fired. Drinking coffee out of someone's coffee mug? That bitch wasn't even there when it happened. She had the fuckin' nerve to write up a report she didn't even witness her doing that shit and on top of that sucking on Valentine's cock made me wanna spit in that bitch's face.

Her writing up that fuckin' report she didn't even witness was like being guilty until proven innocent. It's a classic case of the "The Kahlil Weston Justice System". Going behind closed doors and doing shit like I don't know who was mainly behind it. Then I can't blame her if I knew another nigga was jealous of me.

Valentine drew my wrath when the shit went down with me. To this day I never thought I would find a nigga that was jealous of me. I mean stay trying to find ways to get me fired. I remember once he pulled me in the office for laughing because of an argument he was involved in that had nothing to do with me. He just irrelevantly dragged me in the middle of it. That's a jealous nigga.

As soon as I strike back now he wants to act like he's the victim. Everybody knew he was an asshole I just totally exposed him. I served him his own shit to smell. Niggas don't like to smell their own shit especially when a nigga speaks the truth. I'm gonna sum it up like this…

This nigga swore he was the champ until he got knocked out, pissed on and shitted on. You can't be running around with belts you didn't win. Nobody wants a perpetrator on the throne. When he did finally got me fired he didn't even put me down for the count, better yet he didn't even get a standing eight count.

"WOW!"

People don't like it when you speak the truth. You heard the truth can set you free. Like my aunt once told me there's three sides to every story…

1. Your version!

2. Their version!

3. Then there's the truth!

When you become public enemy number one and you're walking with the bullseye on your back your opinion doesn't mean shit. People think they know shit and they don't. You know Kahlil Weston….

"O.K.!"

"His middle name is Jamal!"

"Yeah!"

You mom's real name is Yvonne!

"I don't call her mom I call her Yvonne!"

Like a broken record I get crucified and persecuted and they don't know shit. Kahlil gets shit dumped on him and my situations get blown up. I need an analysis I tell you what I'm getting Dr. Phil as my shrink. I should be so trusted that I need to be on a dollar bill. Kahlil is so trusted that he needs to be buried to George Washington when he dies because he never told a lie.

"Well that's going a little overboard."

When you're right they got to find a way to say you're wrong. When I'm wrong I'll never hear the end of it. Let me fuck around and say I'm right and nobody wants to hear it. I may hear a bunch of "I'm calling the police" quote fuck the fact that I may be right.

All I hear now is annoying, obnoxious, mouthy, and immature. I talk reckless, I lost my mind because I went to Ancora, and I'm full of it. I may be telling you shit because maybe there's some truth to what I'm saying. If I'm talking that who I killed then you should know that I'm on some non-fiction shit. How can people stay away from me if they still read me? How can you say that you heard enough of me but you still talk me up?

If they hear stories of me then they get off edge because they heard and they know everything. Never mind I don't want to give them a chance because I heard he's crazy. They get paranoid for no reason and I didn't have to do shit to them. Talk about not being able to show off that male sensitivity.

I remember a few years back there was a broad named Ana' Beasley she had to be pushing 50. I ain't gonna lie she had a smoking body but deep down she had real issues. This lady was a total fuckin' nutcase. On top of that this bitch is full of herself.

I was interested in her to and she seemed like she was into it but then this bitch did the unthinkable one day. I was at Labor Ready one day and she had this punk ass nigga to stand up for her. Then this nigga had the nerve to play tough the next day but I put an end to that when I told the nigga lets go around back he got real quiet and told him to quit running his mouth before he tries to cash a check his mouth can't cash. My Kenyatta told me this nigga did it because this bitch tells him that she's afraid I'm gonna do something to her. What had my head fucked up was that I didn't shit to this bitch to warrant that.

When I saw her the next day to see what was up with her and why this nigga tried to shine she didn't even come out the door. My nigga Papi comes outside and he's asking me what's the deal and we're talking and this broad called the cops on me without saying a word. The Stratford cop comes out and starts asking questions about me and runs a warrant check on me and I came up clean. Once she did that I knew the bitch was bad news.

After that happened I just left her the fuck alone. Then this bitch starts running her mouth to other niggas talking shit that if she sees me again she's gonna call the police again. I took that real personal and she knew nothing about me. A week later I was walking home and I walked by Labor Ready and she was locking up and she had the nerve to wave and say hi to me and I stuck up my middle finger and kept walking.

My thinking was like this don't call the cops on me one week and then the next week you want to say hi. I wasn't beat for her anymore do what you been doing. That was some straight hypocritical shit she just proved to me how phony she was.

A month has passed and I was at a point I paid her no mind but here comes the bitch with more drama. Somebody did something to her car and they tried to put the shit on me. One Saturday morning I was walking to Commerce Bank, I walked by

Labor Ready and this Ana starts looking at me from the window, I was like what the fuck is she looking at me so funny I paid it no mind and kept walking.

The next day about 8:30 that morning I was on my way to Philly and when I was walking by Labor Read Papi comes out the door and tried to confront me about something being put on her car. The problem was that I was being blamed and I was left clueless. I then tell Papi that we had a talk about this and that I wasn't going to keep exhausting the situation with this bitch and that I haven't had communication with her since I told him about the middle finger incident and that's all I copped to.

In a way I know it sounds sketchy but on some real for real shit I didn't do that. I know I can do some vicious attacks and be a sneak about it and maybe 5 or six years ago I might've done something like that if you keep rubbing me the wrong way but the thing was that I grew up. When Papi asked me to tell her that I didn't do it she starts copping an attitude and screaming for me to get out and starts bitching about me giving her the middle finger and I was like ok and kept stepping.

Two or three minutes later as I walked down the White Horse Pike I see siren lights and I'm like "oh shit this bitch called the cops" so I tried to take the back roads but unfortunately a Somerdale cop spotted me and drove me back to Labor Ready and I'm being grilled about shit I don't know about. I was pretty pissed and I tried to take the high road for once and I'm being blamed for shit I don't know about.

Then this one cop I look at and I see the nameplate A. Rebecca and I knew from the door who he was. He when asks me questions about me living in Village Green Apartments and I went along with him and I played opossum. He's thinking he knew so much about me and I knew nothing about him. My mini interrogation went on for a few minutes and they let me go. If you know me I had to get one little jab in I told Andrew Rebecca…

"When you see your sister-in-law Hollie tell her I said hi!"

I thought it was funny as fuck to fuck his head but it was my way of saying I know who he is. He thought he was watching me but little did he know that I was watching him watching me. Like I didn't know there was a Rebecca on the Stratford Police. I play chess not checkers.

Back to this broad….anyway! That situation was fucked up and I was to a point I was disgusted with the bitch. Two or three weeks later and I'm walking to Commerce Bank and I'm about a half a mile down the road and Ana is at it again. She claims that I'm around there stalking her and I'm like I can't go nowhere in peace.

This one cop had the audacity to pull over about her. Then he made this one comment that I thought was totally ridiculous asking me do I have a fascination with this bitch. I then told him what part I don't talk to them you don't understand don't ask me about them. I then began to tell the cop that I'm two seconds from filing charges on her for harassment for using 9-1-1 to get to me. I realized that this bitch was full of herself but she's really that fuckin' crazy. I decided to let karma kick her in the ass and that did happened a few weeks later her fuckin' ass got fired.

This bitch really had a complexity problem. She wants to string people along then wants to play them out. I was smart enough to walk away and not to get sucked in. She wants to shoot niggas a dream one minute and lead tem on then pull the rug from underneath them. What I'll never understand that she called the cops on me for no reason and I didn't do nothing to her to deserve that. So much for being a nice guy that girls claim they can't find. It taught me that she's not trustworthy.

When I see Ana today I pay her no mind. She's irrelevant to me because she's a fucked up individual. Obviously for some odd reason she had some sort of mysterious animosity towards me. I know not to trust her. Who knows we can go to the movies, I'll tell her I'm going to the bathroom and the minute my back is turned she'll probably pull out the cell phone and say that I followed her to the movies and I could be her date but that's how fucked up she is.

What I learned in life is that everyone lies. Including me at the same time loyalty and honesty to my friends is important to me. I also have to learn that people don't care. I find it humorous that people are always shooting off shit about me and when I give them the dirtier treatment all that other shit goes out the window what they did. Some people want to hide the truth and at the same time it's not over to me until I bring out the truth and they don't want to handle it.

Four Hours of Freedom

(Chapter Fifteen)

You want to hear some fucked up shit the way the shit went
down. Here's the lowdown...February 25, 2003

I'm finished doing a 364 day jail term over some stupid shit I did over a fuckin' dollar. I get called bag-n-baggage at 10:30 am. I'm souped and I'm happy that I'm happy to be out of jail. I just want to go home and relax. It's time to get my life back on track.

I get downstairs to admissions and it was the beginning to an unpleasant day. It starts off by me not having my clothes. I thought they lost my clothes but they didn't. I go to sign out my property and the guy who does the property in the window asked me the name on the receipt and it read Annaphine Weston.

"Yeah! That's my mom," I answered.

"Well she signed out your property last year," he tells me.

"Oh alright!" I exclaimed.

I take a little walk down the street. Well a long walk. I have fucked up clothes looking like a homeless bum. The county issued me these clothes. I'm walking down Broadway to the unemployment office. I get to the unemployment office to see if I can get my claim re-opened. I get some jacked news. I couldn't get it back.

So I said fuck it. I made a phone call to Angela. She seemed to be glad to hear from me. I told her what happened, I was gonna call her back but I didn't. The next thing I did was call the Philadelphia Daily News. I called my mom's extension but I got her voicemail. The next best option was to call Jenice and to see if she was working that say. Jenice picks up the phone.

"Where's my mom Jenice?" I asked.

"She took off from work today. How are you doing?" she asked.

"I'm in a bad fuckin' mood," I answered.

"Oh you are. I know she's eager to hear from you. You should give her a call," she says.

"Are you positive?" I asked, "I haven't spoken to anybody since July. I don't have the slightest clue what is going on."

"I know she wants you home. Call her. I know she's eager to hear from you. I got to go," she says.

I hung up with Jenice and my instincts told me don't call my mom. Instead I called Tracy's but the number wasn't working. It was about 1:15 pm. I walked to Baird Blvd. and when I got there I don't see any cars that looked familiar to me. I began to feel that something wasn't right. I knock on the door and this Hispanic guy answers the door.

"Hi?! I'm looking for the people that live here. They been here for years?" I asked looking quizzical.

"They moved last year," he tells me.

"Huh! I'm sorry to disturb you," I said.

"That's O.K!" he says.

I began to get worried. I went to Dominic's house. My mind was a little zoned. I had no idea what was going on. I get down the streets to Dominic's and his mom answered the door.

"Hey!" Ms. Kay says.

"Hi! Umm! I need to ask you a question. They don't live there anymore?" I asked.

"Yeah! They got evicted last year," she answered.

"Huh!" I looked puzzled when she said that.

"You didn't know that? Where have you been all this time?" Ms. Kay asked.

"In jail!" I answered.

"Kahlil!" Ms. Kay says, "You need to stop."

Ms. Kay continues....

"All I know is that Tracy has his own place in Cramer Hill and his parents live in Pollocktown," she says.

My next guess is if they lived in Pollocktown and I remember Tracy wrote me a letter that he was working in Cream School. My next guess was to talk to Ms. Rowe. I asked Ms. Kay what time was it and she tells me 2:20. I got up to Cream as fast as I can.

I get up to Mt. Ephraim Ave and Carl Miller Blvd. I spot Tracy's dad. I ran him down and I dashed down Tioga Street and popped up on Mulford Blvd. luckily Tracy's dad parked his car and I caught up with him. He spotted me, he told me that came up to the school to pick up Terrell and Nicloette from Cream.

"Hey!" he said

I'm out of breath.

"Yeah! We moved about eight months ago. Tracy has his own lace in Cramer Hill. What brings you up here?" he asks.

"A friend of mines works up here. When Tracy wrote me last year he mentioned that he was working up here," I answered.

Mr. Clark says, "Tracy was working up here last year. He hasn't worked since the end of the school year. You just got out?"

"Yeah!" I answered, "About a couple of hours ago."

"You didn't know about the eviction?" he asked me.

"Nobody told me anything. I haven't spoken to anyone since July. I haven't seen or heard anyone for several months. I have no idea what's going on," I said.

"Have you spoken to your mom?" Mr. Clark asked.

"Like I said before. I haven't spoken to anybody. I don't know anything," I told him.

"Give me your phone number and I'll have Tracy give you a call," he says.

I gave him my phone number and I went inside Cream School. I went to Ms. Rowe's classroom. I see Ms. Rowe and I spot her and I pull her outside the room. Then Ms. Rowe starts jumping down my back for sneaking the bus driver. I'm like…

"O.K! O.K! I made a mistake you're sounding like my parents. I need to talk to you about a friend of mines."

"Who?" Ms. Rowe asked.

"Tracy Clark! Ms. Debbie!" I answered.

"I don't know who you're talking about," Ms. Rowe answered.

"Come off it Ms. Debbie. You remember Tracy Clark he worked here last year. He told me in a letter how he met you. He knows I know you," I said.

"Oh! You're talking about your godbrother Tracy. I remember him now. He was working here briefly. He was telling me that he was engaged and the whole nine," she says.

"I know! I know! He also thought that you were kind of cute," I said.

Ms. Rowe smiled. I couldn't get any information out of her and I asked about Brittany. Brandi? Well…screw her. We can't stand each other anyway. When it became evident that I ran out of leads. I decided to go home and face the music. Boy was I in for a surprise.

I use the PATCO ticket that the jail gave me and hopped on the speedline. I got off at the Lindenwold Station and proceeded to Voorhees. As I walked up White Horse Road, I looked up to my left I saw a Voorhees and a Stratford policeman talking in front of the Coup. I assumed something happened and I went along with my business.

When I get to the Wawa on white Horse and Burnt Mill Road Patrolman Struckus pulled up in back of me. He drove up with my back turned and he motioned me over. I said…

"Hi! How are you? Look if you have a warrant I just got out of jail a few hours ago, and I don't have the slightest clue what's going on."

Struckus says, "Just show me the papers, you just got out?

"Yes!" I cried, "I'll show you the papers."

As I was pulling out the papers all of a sudden a handful of Voorhees squad cars came up on me. Then faggot ass Del Palazza came out and just started running up on me and started the bullshit.

"You do have a warrant Kahlil," he said.

"For what? A little fine?" I asked.

"No! You have a warrant for violation of final restraining order," Del Palazza said.

"Wait a minute this is a joke right? I just got out of jail a few hours ago. I didn't even make it home. Stop playing!" I exclaimed.

"I assure you Kahlil this isn't a joke. You called your mom's job. You were hollering screaming at your mom's friend saying where's my fuckin' mom at," Del Palazza said all arrogantly.

"You don't know what you're talking about. I got out four hours ago. I spoke to my mom's friend Jenice but I didn't say what you think I said. Get your facts straight when you speak because I didn't say anything like that," I said.

"Maybe you didn't hear what I said. You called her job and you were hollering and screaming to her over the phone to your mom's friend. Her friend called your mother and your mother called us and you're going right back to jail," Del Palazza said.

"What?" I asked.

"You're just finish doing a 364 and you're going right back," he says.

"Get the fuck outta here," I said.

The cops cuffed me. I was only out four hours and my black ass got locked right back up. I was baffled; the same day I get out of jail I'm getting locked right back up. I guess that was my get out of jail present from my own mother. I hope that bitch is proud of herself. You would think that your mom would be glad to see you home but goddamn she was up to no good.

I went to court a week later and all of a sudden the charges were mysteriously dropped. Well the courts didn't have a case against me. They said that I didn't talk to my mom therefore the restraining order was never violated. Then my mom lied in court and said that she got Tracy's address out in Cramer Hill and that I could stay with him.

Later that night I went to Tracy's. Tracy told me how my mom was bragging and gloating about how she got me thrown back in jail. I was still puzzled because I didn't learn about what was the real reason why my mom was running her mouth that I couldn't move back home until I learned the truth.

I then learned of the set up about a couple of weeks later. Tracy and I were in a deep discussion and we were talking about the controversial image that I carry. He then realized the shit that people say about me is fabricated and he didn't understand why I get a bad rap the way I do. I told Tracy…

"Oh my god you sound like Antoinette."

Tracy told me about a Christmas card that my mom sent him over the holidays. I saw the card and it had her name and signature on there. I then began to have flashbacks about what my mom said to the public defender in court a couple weeks before I saw that card. If my mom said that she got Tracy's address a couple of weeks ago then why did she send Tracy a Christmas card and Christmas was 2 ½ months ago.

I asked Tracy, "When did your family get evicted again?"

"June 26th. I remember that day like the back of my hand it was very unpleasant," Tracy answered.

"And she made the comment in early July that I couldn't move back home. How ironic; now it makes sense," I said to Tracy, "Dude! She set us up."

Tracy didn't understand how and I had to tell him. I told him how my parents knew all along and didn't even tell me when I was in jail all that time. I told that my mom has the audacity to send him a Christmas card and not one to his other family members. He shook his head because he realized that my mom took advantage of him and his families' misfortune. Now the world can understand why I'm writing up chapter called "Finishing What You Started."

TELLING SHAY
(SKIT)

Kahlil: Hey Shay I got something to tell you.

Shay: What's up?

Kahlil: I already know it's irrelevant but I rather tell you now even though it's too late.

Shay: Say it!

Kahlil: I had a talk with my friend Kenyetta recently and I asked her who did she think I loved the most and she said you.

Shay: For real?

Kahlil: Well yeah! I know that you have a man and a child but I felt like I was entitled to tell you.

Shay: What about the other girl you liked?

Kahlil: I haven't seen her in almost a year and I still care for her. The real deal was that it was you and it will be that way. I just want you to be happy.

Shay: What about that other girl from school?

Kahlil: Hell no! That's been over. I'll tell you I'll never go down that path again. I hope you don't get upset with what I said.

Shay: Mmm-Mmm! I got to go anyway I'll check out your disk when I get a chance.

Kahlil: O.K. I'll see you around.

I Shot the Pope

(CHAPTER SIXTEEN)

I'm sitting up in Ancora because I was acting like a dumb nigga. I had to go and commit another mean deed to add to my resume of felonies I've committed. Now I did the ultimate sin. I would be crucified by Pontius Pilate would want me crucified in front of the Jews for my sins committed of the father.

It's always The World's Greatest Writer and the great Kahlil Weston is at it again and not afraid to take on what I do and what I say and I wanted to be the hearlded supervillian. Now I'm sitting like a goose because they finally caught up with me. I think I might've gone too far this time and it's pretty obvious I jumped off the deep end.

I did an act of severe violence that has me in jail again. They had a parade for the pope when he came to the Delaware Valley. You should've seen the way the people went to the streets when he came around. He was waving to the crowd. People bowed gracefully in front of him and cried when they saw the man they idolized.

My mind was thinking about a way to get myself into some new shit and I thought about it like if I shot the pope would that give me the credibility to let the world know that I'm a force to be reckoned with. It was the perfect opportunity to show that I am a villian and I have wicked intentions to start some shit.

Now that it was made up that I needed to find a way to shoot the pope I needed to set up operation and I decided to do it on the Philadelphia Newspaper Inc. building and set up shop to shoot him up. I had these visions that I was Lee Harvey Oswald and the pope was JFK and that I could see myself shooting for his head and watching his head explode in the car and watching his fuckin' brain fall out and onto somebody's lap and making him brain dead and unlike Oswald I wouldn't have got caught because I'm too intelligent for that shit to get caught.

I'm not into idolizing but I do have a pretty bad obsession that I needed to kill somebody and I didn't kill anybody in my last book but I will this time. I had the strategy mapped out and how I was going to do it. I knew and always said that John Paul II was about to croak and I considered it my time to shine and get the attention I deserved.

I'm too broke to go out to Vatican City to do it. I was itching to get him to come to American soil and when I got my opportunity to kill him. I got my rifle from when I sniped people from the Wes Allen Muhammad chapters and decide to put it to use.

That morning I got up thinking about what I had ahead of me and how I was gonna do it. Of course I got goosebumps because I don't know how it would go down. You know me being me that I want to start some shit and that I get a high out of doing it and not getting caught and on to the next shit.

I got the snipermobile out of impoundment and went to the roof of the Philadelphia Newspaper Inc. and went to the top roof. I drove over to Philly and was able to get clearance from the security at the paper and i didn't even get my equipment checked when I went to the top of the roof and set up my shit and just waited patiently to start some mayhem.

Just to kill time so I just pulled out some Playboys and began to read and look but I get antsy and impatient because I want to shoot him. I had that mind of a killer and that look in my eye that I wanted it done. My vicious side was unlocked and I knew that I wasn't taking any pity.

I watched the parade down Broad Street as everyone was happy to see him. I sat there and patiently waited to see him parade down the street and I got that hungry look in my eye to get him. He was getting into range and I can sense I was itching to shoot. I treated it like any other person I want to kill I just get nervous and that rush goes into my body.

I look at him on my target and I felt like O.K. I'm ready to do it. He was there and I was like fuck it let it go Wes and turn this golden day into chaos. You don't think that because I see a famous world leader that I won't take an aim at him too? Time for some mayhem.

"Pop! Pop! Pop!"

One shot! Two Shot! Like shooting ten little Indians. I heard the crowd scream in total shock and you know what I'm thinking it's time for me to get out of dodge. I saw the pope collapse and from the magnifying glass on my rifle and I know that I didn't shoot him in the head.

I saw the pope collapse inside of the car. It made me satisfied but I had to get the fuck out of dodge. I got out alright. Off the roof and I try to get downstairs and was hoping to get out O.K. I was flying down the steps. I didn't even think about gathering my shit I'm trying to get out of dodge and not get caught.

As I ran down the steps it was like the FBI was already tracking down where the shots came and they even got the dogs to trace down the shooter. It was a little bit of a rush going through my body but that's how you feel when you get nervous.

Before I could make my escape the police barricaded the area and try to find the guilty culprit who did it. You know that I'm not the type of person to turn myself over and act like I did it so I left my equipment behind because I knew that I couldn't carry that shit downstairs because security would get suspicious.

By the time I got downstairs and they have the police tracing where the shot came from and the helicopters were flying all over the place. The Philadelphia Police Force was all over like a swarm of bees. They rushed in the Daily News and began talking to security.

I over heard them say that they think that the shots that came out was from somewhere in the vicinity in the building but they couldn't pinpoint where. I left and was able to get out the building but one of the police officers looked me in the eye and the way he looked it was like he was trying to have me look like the suspect. I felt the ice water go through my body.

I was able to make it out by the skin of my teeth but I knew they would be looking for me hot and heavy and I knew it was gonna be sealed as tight as they don't want planes flying into the Pentagon zone. You know being who I am and the swagger and the confidence that I can carry around of course I think I can get away with it.

The cops got real suspicious and a description of me was sketched and before I even made it across the bridge back to New Jersey to think I can get away with it. When I drove over the bridge I heard it all through the radio that the pope was shot and they had a description of the person who did it. The description didn't seem to fit me but you know how you think they won't get you but in the long run they do.

I'm at the end on the jersey side of the Benjamin Franklin Bridge and the Delaware Port Authorities were there to greet me. They even said my name....

"Mr. Weston?!"

"What?" I asked.

Not much more had to be said and words were exchanged and they traced my background about all the evil deeds I've done in my lifetime but I was never bought to justice. What more can I say? I knew the police had it out for me.

I was caught and they took me into the station for questioning. I had the mayor and the chief of police give me the third degree about my actions. I guess the snipermobile has been seen around shooting scenes once too many.

They told me I was pretty intelligent how I mapped out my strategies and the way I get out and escape and that I'm clever for a criminal. I gave them this arrogant smug and didn't say shit when I was being interrogated. I had Commissioner Johnson telling me that the community was in an uproar about shooting a peaceful man like the pope.

The Vatican was in total shock and the media and the world looked worldwide as the Wesman is now embattled in a case of shooting the pope. My name was all over the Television screen all over the world. They even traced my name back when I was calling myself and taking the name Wes Allen Muhammad.

I admit I did it for the publicity and the attention and that I was carrying out Lucifer's evil deed about proving that evil always triumphs over good. It was my wicked plan that I was carrying out because I had the devil in my eyes and that you had to prove that I did it because you don't know if I did it or not.

Mayor Street remembers me from my cousin Lorina Marshall-Blake's wedding. He was disgusted by the course of my actions and he knew I was raised with better common sense than that and I knew better and I didn't see it like that. I told him.....

"I had my reasons to go after the pope. If I had it my way I would shoot the president. It seems like I have issues with politicians or very powerful people and I seem like I'm pretty jealous of them. It's been a little different for me I just have it in me to cause some sort of treachery. I guess it's in the genes since I'm half Indian and that blood of the crazy horse made me snap. Of course you know that I like to be held being accountable for my actions."

They didn't understand why did I do it and I caught a case but I requested to have my ass go back to Camden County Jail and face the music for the event of my sadistic actions. They didn't want to run the case and the trial in Philadelphia they chose Camden because of the publicity of the case.

They said I was being extradited to Camden and that I couldn't stay here in Philly and the Camden County Sheriff's Dept. was coming with the van to come and haul my black ass away. Of course the whole world was in a fuckin' uproar and they had to put a bulletproof vest on me because they didn't know who was out to get the Wesman and I guess the enemies I made wanted to see me finally have the book thrown at me.

Well at least I got Philadelphia some attention all over the world and how they had to rush the pope to the hospital and that his condition was in critical but stable condition. I was already facing the fact that I was facing attempted murder charges for trying to kill him which I was prone and I felt like I was destined to do.

I had to be the one that killed him and of course I failed. I was put in protective custody and the guards saw me coming in and they found out what I did they told me that I had to go mainstream and shoot the pope. Well I felt like I was young enough in me to catch another case. It would've been cool if I got away with it but the bottom line is that I got caught.

I went for arraignment the day after the fuckin' shooting and the judge said my name.

"The State of New Jersey vs. Kahlil J. Weston. Mr. Weston?!" the judge asked.

"Yes!" I answered.

"The charges that you're facing are in Philadelphia but because of the publicity and the population your charges will be heard in the county of Camden," the judge then said.

"I understand," I exclaimed.

The judge told me that my charges were pretty extensive and they charged me from every first degree charge to a fourth degree misdemeanor. The way the media and the judge try to run it I was facing life. You knew I wasn't the patriotic type and I dub myself as a disheartening, black humor spreading criminal.

I get back to P.C. and I see how my name was all over the news from ABC to CNN and even media all over the world was covering my court appearance just to see who Kahlil was. I can't lie I got pretty souped and I thought it was funny and I guess I was being cocky because the world was busy talking about me.

Eventually about that time the pope pulled through and I was ordered out to Ancora for psychiatric evaluation. I went back around the Holly building and was in A ward and my boys Bailey and Garrett were there to welcome me back to Ancora. Garrett got souped and started fuckin' with me bout shooting the pope.

"You had to shoot the pope!" Bailey said.

"You know how Dirty gets down," I said.

"How did you get that off?" Bailey asked.

We went in one of the rooms and I pretty much broke it down. They were hearing how the President was trying to burn me for shooting a religious man and that the Catholics considered me the convict and that a guy like me with all the mayhem that I caused shouldn't be running around ever again.

Then I got that call that the pope wanted to see me face to face. I thought it was a joke when it was first bought to my attention. I was besides myself that the pope wanted to come face to face with the nigga that tried to assassinate him. You know that the attempt failed.

We came face to face and the pope asked me what was the reason that I wanted to take him out and I told him that I wanted to have some personal recognition and I wanted to get it off on his expense. I was a pissed off shooter that wanted to be known and I didn't think I would get caught because I felt invincible.

We sat face to face and eye to eye. I sensed the man wanted to come see the devil's kid and try to turn him into a child of God. When it comes to being the Wesman you don't think like that. I'm just carrying out Satan's evil deeds and that's what I was trying to do.

The pope was a man who was about peace but I'm busy telling John Paul II that I'm a person who likes to spread evil throughout the earth. He was asking for the orderlies to have me placed off the medication and he had it in his heart to forgive me and that we should learn how to forgive. Knowing me you know I wasn't beat for that type of shit.

You know that knowing me that I only tell you what I want you to know and what I don't want you to know. I never revealed my intentions and I'm even shocked that he wanted to come face to face with me. I wasn't gonna give him that Flip Wilson being Gearldine Jones catch phrase because I don't need to do that.

I told him that I didn't despise him and that I'm not a bad person I just do bad things and I did have intentions to take him out and it backfired. I wanted to see him dead and I told him that. He gave me blessing and told me that he forgave me and he wanted me to start working on my inner self and to give my life to God. He would be praying for me and ask the court to go lenient on my sentence when I go to court.

I didn't want his pity and I felt like I had justifiable reason to say what I felt and I was sorry that I didn't kill him. I didn't even get my name in the history book that when the kids read about the all and mighty pope they won't learn in grade school that the great Kahlil Weston didn't finish off the job. I felt like I disappointed Lucifer.

Here I am sitting in Ancora trying to see if I'll be found competent to stand trial and that I need to play crazy while these orderlies shoot me up with some drugs and make me look like a walking basehead. The fuckin' judge ain't gonna go for what I say if I try to play crazy.

The questions and answers will always stay and burn inside of me on why I did it and I lost my freedom over it. I got myself in trouble and I can't get myself out of it. I tangled myself in a real sticky spiderweb and I got to find a way to get back to the street and I know I will.

The pope might've forgave me but I still feel this thing for wanting to see him dead. The natural causes got him before the World's Greatest Writer did. Oh well at least I got to see him croak and he did even if it wasn't off my expense.

Being Sinister

(Chapter Seventeen)

You know that I'm intelligent to neutralize your brain and that you just want to talk about my crazy fuckin' mind. Well you thought that I was just hot air and that the hype is real and you backed me in a corner and I came out in a dangerous state of mind. I stimulate your thoughts that you see that the world revolves around me right now.

You thought it was a muthafuckin' gimmick and that I wasn't who I claimed I was until you learn that it was real. I take no prisoners and when I'm speaking in my book I'm the fuckin' sounding board and it can be echoed even if I'm committed in an institution. I've unleashed my alter ego and Delgado wants to come out and fuckin' play.

I keep two people you see one in shadow and one in daylight and it seems that I'm being driven by rage. I totally snapped because I got my reasons and a good soap opera always needs a psycho that's sadistic to talk some off the wall shit and let them think you went off the fuckin' edge.

The ultimate fatal mistake was when they let me out the crazy ward and let me type up a handful of evil things and didn't bother to review my book to see if I needed extra time to be put in a straitjacket and they cut me loose. I have thoughts of terrorizing people by chasing them naked with a chainsaw like I would run around with stiff penis that wants to slip it in between porno star's legs.

So what she has four dicks between her legs are serious enough to talk about having sex with her because there in such perfect shape. Antoinette Ragone is built like a stallion and I would be having fifteen babies with her if Dan and Danny weren't the priority in her life and that goes for both of them.

I'm out to let people know that I'm here and what isn't right for me to say and what will be held against you. Better yet I'd rather be a hated individual instead of being accepted. I'd rather be the heel you didn't like and got cop threats thrown at me. I want you to call the boys in blue. It would give me a reason to be charged with terroristic threats so I can serve out another three years in the New Jersey State prison and waste two years on some retarded shit because I had an ass backwards mother who thinks those cracker ass cops in Voorhees would love to see me in jail.

You know I must be intelligent enough to write a fuckin' chapter about all the fuckin' people I wrote or claimed I killed. I got more sense to say it unlike JFK who lost his mind when his brain fell out of his when it blew up by a gunshot bullet.

You know that I won't be writing shit that sounds too cheesy and I gone crazy because Ancora made me clinically insane and there was never a diagnosis that was declared on me. Yeah I matured but another side has been unlocked and I'm out to taste your blood. It makes you flip and shake in fear that I'm being bold and not vague about starting some shit.

My state of mind has me thinking about what I think is evil and being black. I use words that will hurt you and I get a joy out of it. It's like my mind is a freak of nature. It's that retarded strength in me that brings out the nastiness in me like I'm Kurt Angle trying to break somebody's fuckin' ankle and I get a thrill out of it.

I been going crazy trying to be a goddy two shoes. I'm not about to mellow out and turn in my boy scout badge. I'm itching to start some more shit to give you a reason to say that I'm annoying again. I got a thing for getting under your skin. I'm even asking for you to use the shit I say and write down to see if you can get me indicted.

I had no problem giving my dad a swollen eye and a busted up lip and have no remorse about it. I'm back to being the bad guy it was more fun when all bets were off. You best believe that I want you to shake my hand and acknowledge the fact that the Wesman is just as wicked as they say. There's no two minute warning it just comes at a blink of an eye.

I have this need to be evil and my intentions are pretty wicked and my mind is twisted and it's snapping because I have these Norman Bates flashbacks by wanting to smack some old lady in the head with a shovel. It's like I lost it and my mind went bananas and I'm snapping and skitzing like I have to be the psycho in the soap opera that has to be twisted.

You know that I enjoy being placed in the hotseat. Have my state of mind judged and let them think that I went ballistic. I need to put a gun in my mouth and just blow my fuckin brains out and maybe you may be so fuckin' rid of me. Well newsflash it ain't gonna fuckin' happen in this lifetime.

You hear me going to psychiatric hospitals and it still wasn't big enough to fuckin' hold me. You can tie me up, drug me, and sedate me and it still ain't enough to stop me. You put me in a straightjacket and I'm pulling a David Copperfield by getting out of it.

You heard about that I went to the nuthouse and I really lost some screws well being stuck in there made me lose more. I want to pull out my trustee nine iron and beat Tiger Woods up with it until he stops running around saying that he's 90% Asian. I'll beat the black back into him. Why do tht and his wife is chasing him to beat him up with a golfclub. Yeah evil has a name and his name is Wesman.

I got to keep it by the book if I want to be hated and debated. Back to talking negativly and who I'm out to kill now. I been issuing death certificates and eulogies after I was done using my megaphone to let you fear me.

All my leathal weapons are being used and are at my disposal. I told you when it's all said and done there will be at least ten more people in my book when it's over. I'll be the first to admit that I love to kill people and I talked about it so much that it's actually a fuckin' hobby. If I keep running out of people to kill then mankind would end with me.

Dirty Delgado has come out of me and I'm out for blood. It's into me to start some shit and talk a whole bunch of it. It's like i'm out to touch your soul. I have a better chance of killing you and getting away with it than the Philadelphia Eagles winning the Super Bowl.

This Kahlil is more sadistic than the one you ever met before. I had to tweak my personality that my laugh is more half assed. I guess when you know you're not playing with a full deck you just think evil things and I'm thinking like a villian. Being happy happy joy joy like Ren and Stimpy don't do it for me.

I love being bad. Now the World's Greatest Writer has turned in to the World's Greatest Villian and I think with that black mentality and thinking of ways to be the bad guy. I said enbough shit that I was accued of that would make the FCC want to have me investigated and confiscate my computer just to burn me.

They wanted me locked up and throw away the key and want me to be a dead man walking but I thrive off that because I want you pissed off. I'm totally peed and I want the world to feel it too. I'm not in the type of mood that's foul and I wreak it the grim reaper has just came to reality.

I don't want to tone it down I want to let you know how I feel and who I want to bomb. I've been planning to bomb and destroy since I started this writing shit since 1998. i'm like a baby terrorist that talks about it and I've became a terrorist on paper.

I promote black humor but I'm not up for it. My mind is up for war. That seems to be the mentality that I carry and who dares to challenge what I say or where my frame of mind is. The shit seems better when I talk with negativity. I like it better when you muthafuckers talk about how bad you can't stand me.

Being sinister represents evil and it's right up my alley. I've beat up on enough people in my book and threw darts at so many targets and hit enough bullseyes from the targets I aimed at. I got to be insanely obnoxious and I won't be like the way Steven A. Smith acts.

There are plenty of things for me to start and I got ideas that will make the plot thicken as I come up with more ideas to get thrown in jail. It ain't shit I know what to expect because I've been to jail before. So what else is new if I don't commit something else if I kill somebody else.

They talk about how people finished off Kahlil well Kahlil finished you and that's why my reputation is looked at in a fucked up sort of way. The people that I screwed and tortured after they try to come after me and polish me off they found out that I'm resilent to disrespect you.

I got to show that vicious attitude that got me to where I was. I'm back to make or break and talk about me. I want to prove that I'm more sadistic than Legion of Doom. You couldn't even get the Superfriends or the Justice League to finish me off.

You can't kill me and I ain't ready to join Lucifer and sip christal. If I was a wrestler I'd rather be a fuckin' heel. It's more exciting to be booed and labeled as a troublemaker.

When can I bomb a building and let you know that I'm picking up secrets from bin Laden. Strength rolls in numbers and I'm like a shark when I see blood in the water. I got that mean streak and I don't have a yellow one rolling down my back. If I mellow out it makes my book sound cheesy and I feel like it's my obligation to call Carman Del Palazza a pussy. Yeah I seen and heard that Del Palazza was mad because he was caught with another man's cock in his mouth.

That's why the pussy got the fuck up out of dodge and they ran him out of Laurel Springs. I heard the rumors that he was the gay cop that Laurel Springs didn't want in their jurisdiction. I just pulled his skirt and his card and put his business out there that explains why the pussy breaks his neck to lock me up.

Just don't blink and you might see me strike faster when a snake attacks to swallow a mouse. In my case it's like an anaconda swallowing a zebra. I get fired up when it's time for me to get even. I always find a way to come up with a plan to crush my enemies. I'm still gonna be talking shit when I'm old and sixty. I can be an old man with drool on my lips with a nurse that's as young as twenty and I'll still betaking geritol trying to pinch her ass.

It's so good to be bad and it sucks to be good. Matter of fact I like being bad because I can say the word bitch to anybody I want to lash out at will. I got no fuckin' conscience if I got to lash out like I whipped you at the pillar forty times. I may mock you throw stones at yu and feed you vinegar before I crucify you.

I don't hang you at the cross. I'd rather whip you into submission.

"Heh! Heh! Heh! Heh! Heh!

I'm just practicing my evil laugh right now. I jsut pick with you and start shit just to fuck with you. I'm back to cutting off your balls like Loraina Bobbit and sending them to donation for any she-male who needs a pair nuts. Now it's me talking wit the very sharp tongue that got me in trouble. I got to go back to being infamous and notorious.

It's funny how the tables turn and now it's me being in the hotseat again. I don't burn in it like the world wanted to see when they thought I was fried. I went a little bit or should I say....

"And yes you said!"

Well in any case I should say way over the deep end and now I can't talk about chasing somebody naked with a chainsaw because after a while it gets a little too tired saying the same shit all the fuckin' time. I found new things that make me happy like...

"Calling out a bitch in Franklinville who like to snitch!"

"Sonja wants a cracker!"

"The bitch looks like Polly! How about sneaking another bus driver over a dollar."

"Your pushing it!"

I'm gonna camp out in front of the Tucci's and hold my breathe until Hollie comes back from Maryland.

"KAHLIL!"

The day I do that wil be the day that Mark Tucci will come out with a shotgun and I'll be blown away. I just lost it and I've gone crazy. I need a drink before I kill somebody. My mom looks good to kill right now and by hanging her off the Echelon Glen balcony. All I need is just a good alibi.

All these people hear all the stuid ass rumors that I'm that out of it and that I want to cause harm to myself. Shit well if that's the case than I'll do something to have the bastards to re commit me back to Ancora. Like Public Enemy once said it takes a nation of millions to hold us back. Well it would take a hospital full of orderlies to hold me back.

I had to tune into the tube to find a lot of shit that's going on in the news. In this case I've been making news. All the sinful acts and dasterly deeds and it still hasn't cauhgt up to me and it won't. I got meat clevers stashed in my apartment and if you knock on my door I'm swing it just for paying me a visit.

I got to go back to the real horror that I installed in my enemies just lashing out and verbally beating them until they tap. Even when they tap it's just ain't enough. I'm the nigga that says when I think you have enough. I may keep going until you really get that fuckin' sick of me.

I'll make you so sick and so numb that the name Kahlil Weston leaves that sour taste in your mouth that when my name is bought up that you'll shrug your shoulders. You can't take the fact that you lost. If you lost your best bet is take the high road and walk around with a tail in between your legs.

I got to admit that the shit is more exciting and interesting if I can speak that crazy shit. The shit wouldn't be the same if I wrote a diary acting like I mellowed out. I may be in my thirties but I don't feel like I'm in my thirties and I'm still writing and talking shit like I'm in my twenties again.

This is the type of shit I speak and this is the type of words you hear. I feel like pissing in a urinal and not washing my hand. I would shake your hand and not let you know that my dick was touching my hand. I feel that fuckin' ignorant that I would do something that disrespectful.

I'm in that type of mood to constantly doing and picking up some negative habits. I may spit in your face if you snitch on me for taking dollars off the New Jersey Transit bus. It's the nastinest coming out of me that I'm trying to get you to fight me and I must be breaking my neck if I'm doing some shit like that. If you wipe the saliva off your face then I saw that bitch in you.

There must've been this alarm clock in me that totally went off and the animal in me has been unleashed. I may be dangerous and it ain't the end of the line. I'm not psychoatic but I'm insane when I unlock that personality that's strong enough to cause a split personality.

I guess when I came out my coo-coo of a mom's vagina that I developed a crazy attitude. The trauma was so serious that it was powerful enough for it to happen. When I write these books there's spmething in me that just drives me crazy and it makes me go bananas that I'm speaking this way.

I get these dark moods and it's something for you to know that I'm out to start trouble. It's the dark side of the force and I think I was made out to take Darth Vader's place when Luke struck his hand and being electicuted by the Emperor. I'm trying to rank as one of the greatest villianous writers that ever walked the grace of this earth and in this case the bad guy never loses.

They try to throw me in jail and I always find a way to get out. I say I shot the pope and I escaped the nut ward. I played the character Wes Allen Muhammad and I went down to the Beltway region just to go out and snipe more muthafuckers at will. I committed to many felonies that I have it in my blood to start it again. Now I'm sendig anthrax through the mail and making you fuckin' gasp.

When I feel that type of mood I'm out to seek and destroy. You can play hide and go seek but when I seek my target I see them as a target and I want to sink their battleship. I took it back to the basics and went back to me being me and I ain't sorry that I won't tone it down. You know me as evil and I committed my evil deeds and now the devil can hoist me away.

Twenty Five Dollar Porn Pyramid

(CHAPTER EIGHTEEN)

(Tune of the twenty-five thousand-dollar pyramid)

Matt: Welcome to the twenty-five dollar porn and I'm your host the Reverend Matthew Bonner and let's meet our contestants for this show. First off let's meet our defending champions Tracy and Kahlil.

Tracy and Kahlil (at the same time): What's up Rev.!

Matt: What's up y'all! I see you guys are back to defend your title. So what's been up since I last heard from you guys?

Wes: Well! I've been beating off to so much porn I was about to fuck around and go blind. I got tired of seeing the same scenes like over and over again so I decided I need to stock up on the supply.

Tracy: Me too! I need some new shit. I got tired of looking at the same tapes over and over again too. This time I want some hotter shit then what I won the last time.

Matt: Well that does why you're here and now let's meet your challengers. Tonight your challengers are Tim and Blake. Tim I see you're from Camden and Blake I see you're from Lindenwold. I see you two are new to the game so the rules are like this the team to name the most stars by questions will be our champions. So our defending champions can choose to play or pass so what's it gonna be champs?

Kahlil Weston

Tracy: We'll pass let the amateurs go.

Matt: O.K!...Tim and Blake you have thirty seconds and good luck. You are to discuss porn stars that have been in regular movies or television. Here we go.

(Bell rings)

Blake: She was in Tupac's video "How do you want it" with K-Ci and Jo Jo.

Tim: Heather Hunter!

Blake: Right!...She was in Spike Lee's movie "He got game!" she was a cheerleader. She's been called the nastiest slut in porn.

Tim: Jill Kelly!

Blake: Right again! She's been on the movie "Boogie Nights" she's been called the porn queen pioneer.

Tim: Come on that's Nina Hartley.

Blake: She's been on Jerry Springer, Howard Stern, she did her own mother she fucked Jerry Springer.

Tim: Pass!

Blake: She's been on Howard Stern. She went to the prom with a high school boy. She had her lavia cut down….

Tim: Houston.

Blake: She's been on Brian McKnight's video. She's been called the biggest icon in black porn.

Tim: Pass!

Blake: She did porn when she was under eighteen. She was in Johnny Depp's movie "Crybaby"; she starred in a few other movies.

Tim: Traci Lords!

Blake: Yes! She's been on Jay-Z's video. She has an ass you can't forget her name is after a certain fruit.

Tim: Cherry Lee!

(Bell Rings)

Matt: Five out of seven not a bad score but knowing these guys you would've had to be flawless. Tracy and Kahlil you two are up you guys have the subjects of gangbangs. You two have thirty seconds and good luck!

Wes: She broke the first world sex record by fucking two hundred and fifty one guys in one day...

Tracy: Annabela Chong!

Wes: Yeah! She fucked 551 guys in one day...She's been on Jenny Jones.

Tracy: Spontaneous Xtasy's wacked ass.

Wes: Correct...She did six hundred fifty five guys in one day. She's been on the world's biggest bang off. She went to the prom with a guy once....

Tracy: Houston!

Wes: She did one thousand guys in one day! She was also involved in the world's biggest bang off.

Tracy: Pass!

Wes: She won the title in the world's biggest bang off. She fucked Jerry Springer. She had sex with her own stepmother. She hates Jasmine St. Claire...

Tracy: Kendra Jade!

Wes: Yeah....She did three hundred guys in one day. She's been on Howard Stern. She was a wrestling manager on ECW.

Tracy: Jasmine St. Claire.

Wes: She banged a bunch of guys in Whore Stories. She fucked some of Howard Stern's peoples and it's on a video called "Who wants to be a Vaginal Millionaire?"

Tracy: Annie Andersinn!

Wes: Yeah.

(Bell goes off)

Matt: Six out of seven isn't that bad. Next up is Tim and Blake you two will try to name porn stars from the nineties. You two have thirty seconds and good luck.

Blake: She has big lips and she likes getting it in her ass. She slurped cum off a table in "House of Whores."

Tim: Monique.

Blake: Yes! She was the girl who starred in a movie with Jenna Jameson in a lesbian title.

Tim: Briana Banks.

Blake: Correct! She was Bud Lee's second wife. She's an Asian chick.

Tim: Asia Carrera.

Blake: Correct! Her porn name is pronounced animal. She has a tattoo on her tits and pussy. She likes come in her mouth.

Tim: Anna Malle.

Blake: That's right. She's a porn star that's been rumored about having the package. Her first name is the last name of a famous basketball player.

Tim: Jordan McKnight!

Blake: That's it! She's one of Jenna Jameson's best friends. She was in the lesbian dating game with Jenna on Howard Stern.

Tim: Nikki Tyler!

Blake: Yes! She goes by the name Kendra Jade. What's her real name?

Tim: Kendra Jade Andrews!

Blake: Right! One more. She's Spanish and black. She has a beautiful body. She has a cross tattoo on the top of her breast.

Tim: Tabitha?

Blake: Hell yeah!

(Bell Ring) Ding! Ding!

Matt: Good job! That round you were seven out of seven is excellent. That brings your score up to twelve to six and Mr. Weston and Mr. Clark is up next you two have thirty seconds. You guys will talk about girls with small boobs and a big butt. Good luck!

(Bell sounds off)

Tracy: She has no boobs but a fat ass and she's white but she stars in a lot of black movies.

Wes: Lana Sands!

Tracy: You know it! She's our personal favorite when she wears the glasses and she looks cute as hell. She has those real pretty eyes.

Wes: Stephanie Swift!

Tracy: Terueee!!!!! This is a two part question the only twins in porn.

Wes: Mocha and Chocolate.

Tracy: Give us the double. She has a big ass and you know she's one of my favorite actresses. She has long hair and sucks a mean dick.

Wes: Janet Jacme!

Tracy: Jack another one up for the bad guys. She had a jheri curl. She was considered a black goddess before the nineties came into effect.

Wes: Angel Kelly.

Tracy: O.K. She does straight girls. She is a lesbian to her name.

Wes: Felecia

Tracy: She has red hair. You should know she's one of your types.

Wes: Brittany O' Connell.

Tracy: That's it!

Ding! Ding! (Bell sounds off)

Matt: Seven for seven isn't bad for you two either that brings your total up to thirteen. Now it's time for our challengers to turn up the heat on you two. With the score thirteen to twelve these are the last questions for this round. This is a freestyle round so you guys will have to answer porn stars from all generations thirty seconds and good luck….

(The bell goes off)

Blake: The fat man.

Tim: Ron Jeremy!

Blake: Right. Her letter begins with the fourth letter in the alphabet.

Tim: Dee!

Blake: She's a bony Asian chick with a boob job.

Tim: Kobe Tai.

Blake: Uh huh! She was one of the first Asian girls out there in porn she has her own website.

Tim: Mimi Miyagi!

Blake: Yes! She 's Jody Watley's little sister. She dated Kid Rock! She's been in every black video known to man.

Tim: Midori!

Blake: O.K. She's Bud Lee's first wife. She's Indian!

Tim: Hyapatia Lee!

Blake: Correct! She named herself after her eyes. Another word for black, she has huge tits.

Tim: Ebony Ayes!

Blake: Yeah!

Ding! Ding! (The bell goes off)

Matt: Nice job fellas! The score is nineteen to thirteen! Tracy and Kahlil, you have thirty seconds to guess all seven questions to retain your title. This subject in porn is also a freestyle for you two also. Thirty seconds good luck!

(The bell goes off)

Tracy: She's been in porn back when we were teens. She has a nice body. She was in an X-Files episode several years ago.

Wes: Ashlyn Gere.

Tracy: Right! We said she's wacked. She can't fuck. She has blonde hair for a black chick.

Wes: Fonda French.

Tracy: Correct! She use to be a singer before she got started in the porn business. She named herself after a country.

Wes: India.

Tracy: Right on! She has big titties. She did a bathroom skit on the Man's Show once.

Wes: Brittany Andrews.

Tracy: Three more! One of your favorites. She's been a correspondent in the E! Wild On shows. The white girl with the big ass. Not Antoinette but......

Wes: Serenity!

Tracy: She named herself after a luxury car. It's a souped up version of a Toyota.

Wes: Lexus.

Tracy: One more! She's one of your favorites too. She's a redhead but she use to be a blonde. She was in Face Jam...

Wes: Kylie Ireland!

Ding! Ding! Ding! (The bell goes off)

Matt: That's it you guys retain the title!

Wes: Oh shit! We're going to get more porn I'm souped.

Tracy: I want nothing but black. Yeah boy! I want all Janet.

Matt: Today your prize is going to a free trip to the East/West porn convention when it comes to town.

Wes: Hell yeah!

Matt: Would you like to go for a year supply of porno tapes in our bonus round?

Tracy: You're goddamn right we do.

Matt: O.K. come over to the chair and let's get the round started. Once again you have thirty seconds good luck.

(The bell goes off)

Tracy: She was in Junior Mafia's "Get Money" video

Wes: Vanessa Del Rio!

Tracy: Yeah! She's not Vanessa but she has the same last name except Del she's Spanish.

Wes: Alicia Rio!

Tracy: You hit the nail right on the head. She's downloaded on the Internet. She has her own website and she has a guy's name.

Wes: Danni Ashe!

Tracy: Alright! She's been in videos during the early nineties. She has her own video production company. Her last name is the twenty-sixth letter in the alphabet...

Wes: Ona Zee!

Tracy: Good! Not a cat but a baby cat!

Wes: Kitten!

Tracy: My girl. Big ass. Crackhead size titties!

Wes: Obsession.

Tracy: She use to do porn. She named herself after a city in Wisconsin. She had dark hair.

Wes: Madison.

(The bell goes off)

Matt: That's it you guys win the bonus round.

Tracy: Hell yeah!

Matt: Let the celebration begin you guys win a year supply of porno tapes of actress of your choice.

Wes: I'm in porn heaven.

Matt: Thank you for tuning in. I'm the Reverend Matthew Bonner and tune in next time when we play the Twenty-Five Dollar Porn Pyramid.

(The song to the twenty-five thousand dollar pyramid)

Wes: I'm gonna start another chain of porn shops with my tapes.

Tracy: Tah! Hah! Hah!

I Have a Boyfriend
(Skit)

Kahlil: Sonja! I have this real funny feeling that Hollie knows the truth. I don't know whether she knows or not but I feel it in my bones that she knows.

Sonja: You think she knows?

Kahlil: I think she does know and I think it's gonna go down tonight.

(Forty-five minutes later)

Sonja: You're leaving?

Kahlil: Yeah! I'm going home.

Sonja: I like your earrings. How did you pierce them?

Kahlil: Oh! I pierced them myself. It took about ten minutes. (Interrupted)

Hollie: Kahlil?

Kahlil: What's up?

Hollie: I need to talk to you. It's pretty important.

Kahlil (talking in his mind): I got a funny feeling that she knows the truth.

Hollie: It has to do with the bear that you gave me. It is important.

Kahlil: Uh! Say what you got to say.

Hollie: You know I have a boyfriend?

Kahlil: Um! Uh! Yeah! But…

Hollie: I just wanted to get that straight because I was hearing a lot of things.

Kahlil (talking in his mind): She knows! She knows! What am I gonna do? Aww man!

(Five minutes later)

Kahlil: I want to talk to you for a minute.

Hollie: What?

Kahlil: Why did you say that?

Hollie I was just hearing a lot of things and I wanted to get that straightened out.

Kahlil: Look when I gave you that teddy bear I gave it to you because I meant it. I really do care about you.

Hollie: Look! I do believe that you are a decent guy and I think it was nice but I… well…I got to go. (Walks away)

Kahlil (talking in his mind): This is not fair and I cared.

Prove Me Wrong

(CHAPTER NINETEEN)

You remember back when you're in grade school and you write a letter to girl that you like. You're just head over heels in puppy love with them. You're shy about because you don't want to be embarrassed then eventually temptation wins you over and you have to get it out of you.

Tell somebody that you're working on a book and it's kind of autobiographical and you think they're interested in your writing but they're not. They wanna find out shit and see what's your interest in the pursuit.

"It goes something like this".....

I had this diss waiting. You wanna play the friend act and beat around the bush. I know your little secret and what you're up to. I'm settling a score that you wanted to force my hand into. All because of a chapter I wrote about somebody, I had feelings for and you got all jealous.

Two days after I wrote that chapter of what I was feeling for her here you come. You got mad because it wasn't you that got the attention and you were seeing her from a totally different angle all this time without anybody knowing. I said it before and I'll say it again. Your role wasn't to say shit about what I felt for her and what I wrote. You wanna play spoiler well I feel like raining in on your plan. Yeah!...I'm on some fly in the ointment shit.

Let's reminisce about the chapter I gave her that night. I gave it to her because I wanted her to know how I felt. She already knew what I was doing because I let her know what I was doing right after the crush was revealed to her and I was going through a healing process after the sting wore off. Since she knew that I liked her and it was no longer a secret I just opened up my feelings for her. I didn't plan on talking about it unless she wanted to but you had to add your two little pennies into the mix. The only person that I probably would've opened up to amongst the peers we knew would've been Sonja, Angela, and Antionette that's it.

You, her, Gary, and Antoinette got to Antoinette's house that night and y'all got the talking and she was reading what Wes wrote. I guess she was flattered about what I said and you took the chapter from her. While she caught giggles your lip tightened up. Probably all pissed off you couldn't say shit that I wrote. Gary mentioned something about Kahlil getting it published and it made you sweat.

I took over the room that night and I wasn't even there. Antoinette told her I had no control over my feelings for her. Any girl who knows the meaning of really liking someone probably agreed with what Antoinette said.

The girl probably thought….

I can't believe Kahlil just said that about me.

Well buddy I did say it. I ain't sorry I said it and it's nice to know she liked it. You wanna travel through the mind of a mastermind. That's the way Dirty Delgado gets into the book. You can act like I'm delusional but you know I'm speaking the truth. Is anybody hearing what the Wes Daddy Mack is saying?….I just got warmed up and it's time for this little weasel to burn in the hotseat.

You wanna come up to me and talk about how nice my penmanship is but you were on a conniving act. You asking me about the book I write and I was summarizing the first one. I talked about staying in the timeframe of the first one I gave to Sonja but you slipped up.

As soon as you said about me updating the second one it didn't take long for me to put two and two together. I knew you read what I wrote because she was the only one who had the new shit I wrote. She was the only one I showed the new stuff to. I showed the copy of the chapter I wrote about her.

You wanna say…

"Well you know she has a boyfriend!"

This just in….

"I KNOW YOU FUCKIN' IDIOT!"

I asked you how did you know and you said you took the copy from her. I guessed she liked it so much it pushed a button in that baldhead of yours. You see my friend my little secret is no longer a secret and I reached the crossroads where my feelings lied and I put how I felt out there. I had no fear about what I was feeling. I was in a everything to gain and nothing to lose situation.

Then you wanna say you were just looking out. Sure you were! You had your own agenda. You left a scent I picked up on. If you don't remember maybe I'll remind you about a conversation you had with Steven West the day you confronted me. Steve was sitting next to me and I found out your dirt.

Fifteen minutes after you spoke to me you spoke to Steve and she came walking by. You must've had on some cologne on because she said you smelled good and kept walking. You went to Steve's ear and started saying…

"Yo! She thinks I smell good! That's a good thing isn't!"

I was warned that you liked her but that clue became evident.

You're always out your seat and looking around when she walks by. I didn't realize you're that strung and in love with her. If she didn't know then well she knows now because she's reading it. Now I see why you slyly approached me that day because I threw a monkey wrench in your plans. You probably went home that night saying….

"That goddamn Weston!"

You approaching me that night stuck in my mind. I asked Antoinette did she read something I gave to her buddy. She said yes and asked me did I mind her reading her what I wrote and I said no, whoever she showed it to was up to her. I will admit that I was pretty embarrassed and it was in a good way. A Blackman would've blushed the way it was accepted. If she shows it to the world then I want to let the world know how I feel.

You had plans for years to have her for you. You asking Steve that question became evident that you're goal was endanger. You had a better chance at getting a girl on the Internet than getting with her. You got jealous because I grab the attention and you didn't. You were better off deferring to me.

I know you were busy hating on me. What did you think she was just another pretty face? You just thought you would look good on her arm. You have to intrigue her by being versatile. She knows I have a wild side but I do have a caring side to me. You have to be willing to adjust to her but you acting like when I was arguing with her was gonna better your chances.

As far as I'm concerned I have a bone to pick with that other joker named Dave. He was hung and strung doing the same shit you do. Dave was already over the edge and it drove him nuts to see me talking to her. He lacked the character and personality I have and so do you. That's why I said I do what I do best and that's doing the unpredictable.

As you see my friend. I'm considered an outlaw and an allegiance of writers want to know about the shit I say and you're the goose out of the ducks in the pond. I tell her what I want her to know and I personally don't care if you knew. She knows she's the only woman that drives me crazy. She knows I'm a heel but she knows I'm not as bad as assholes like you portray.

If you haven't learned how impulsive I can get. I can be so wicked not you, her, Antoinette, Gary, Sonja, or her mama can do shit to stop me. Putting you in the book was an idea; writing it down was an impulse. The fun part is submitting the hard details for supporting my facts.

I don't really worry myself about you because she knows I'm pretty intelligent to put you on the backburner. Just to downgrade you, I know how to whew her you don't. I know when she's mad at me and you're just sitting there like an opportunist…that was evident when she called me an asshole at The Grove Inn" but I'll talk to her to work it out. She usually wins because I know how to defer.

Let's talk about that night at the Grove. As much kissing up you did who was she mad at if it wasn't the boyfriend. It wasn't you it was me. She was mad at me because I didn't speak to her. She got pissed off at me because I didn't but her a drink. The night that happened something was going on in that pretty little head of hers. Her anger towards me carried over that Monday.

When you saw us arguing that day I saw you smirking. You were probably grinning hoping that she wouldn't speak to me anymore. I don't think it was going to reach that point yet. You must got me confused with the guy she calls the boyfriend. I don't treat her that bad. I may do some crazy shit but I know when I do know how to speak my mind and most importantly the truth. At least I go out my way to apologize to her.

While it's on my mind don't you have a girlfriend? Why are you hatin' on Wes? I didn't write a chapter about your girl but who knows she may be a bone I may have buried in my backyard. Ahh!!! I'm lying! Don't sleep because Jody might be creepin' with her. Acting like you and your girl are on the outs and you're just pretending.

I just pulled your card boy. If she asked you to double date you would back out because we all know who was the girl you really wanted on your arm. You're that mad because she wasn't your date. You may have fooled your other buddies but you didn't fool me. As I see it the girl on your arm is just a masquerade. You're just covering up to make sure your tracks don't show.

I think you're afraid of rejection. Suffering pain is a part of life. I got shot down more than Diallo got shot up in New York. You've been interested since the day you laid eyes on her. You cock block anyone that stands in your way. That's why I don't tell you shit I'm not gonna let you tarnish my bad boy reputation.

What's the difference between me and you? Let's see:

- ☐ I'm annoying, you're quiet!
- ☐ I'm the bad guy; you're the good guy!

□ I'm black, you're white!

□ She knows I like her and now she knows you like her!

□ I talk a lot of shit, you're full of shit

□ I got a menacing alter ego named Dirty Delgado…NUFF SAID!

Just because you had to stick your nose in chapters not even mentioned about you and this is what you get. You can't say shit because you know it's true. Now you may think I see you as a threat but I actually don't. You're as harmless as a roach with can of raid sprayed on his back. You provide little competition for me.

Even people agree with me that you had no business saying shit. I don't believe you were looking out for her because you weren't. I don't buy that crap for one minute. You're not fooling anybody the night you read it made me realize I flattered her. Nobody expected Wes to woo her the way I did.

Who did you confuse me for her boyfriend or Dave? In case you forgot who I am my name is Kahlil Jamal Weston. The same Kahlil Weston who will character assassinate you like blood on O.J.'s knife. Why don't you just fess up and tell her how you feel. You're afraid she'll embarrass you?

I bet in the years you've known her I bet you didn't do one thing to make her feel special. Well I did and you wish you had the testicles like I did. I exposed you and I understand that you're hiding the fact that you're hiding the truth. You're just another dude who underestimates my intelligence.

You liked her longer than I known her. I just came out of nowhere and blew right by you. It would make your day if you heard her say….

"I hate Kahlil for everything he's done."

Uh! Sorry it ain't gonna happen. I made no secret of how I feel about her. Remember when you thought I liked Angela?…I just played you along to see if you would find out who she really was. I had your head scrambling for days and then I told you who it was you got all defensive and then you want to say….

"Oh! She likes Brian!"

I ain't got no beef with him but you started saying shit that she'll never like you. You can't flatter her and you're not her boyfriend. All y'all had the deck stacked against me before she even knew. I guess it was better for me because I felt no pressure because nobody ever thought I would make her feel like platinum. I wanted to shock the world and I began to feel the tables turn.

I guess because I'm a different shade and it didn't seem like a guy like me could do what I did. I just shift gears on all of y'all. You don't have that in you. You're not on my level when it comes to her and you damn sure don't have my intelligence. If she asks you about this just be a man and you can't deny what I said because I speak the truth.

Boiling Point

(CHAPTER TWENTY)

At times I want to speak out about a lot of shit. I hold back because I'm the nigga that has to take the hit. It's building up for sometime and it threw me to a point I wanted to be thrown into a fit. I don't want to hear Yvonne says she loves me because it sounds like a sack of shit. I'm not getting singled out because you really don't know what was the real deal behind the shit.

Here I go. Let me blow off some stress. I get my aggression out that way. I'm short on tolerance and my fuse is lit. Somebody or someone had to do something that just made me totally react. You want to know why don't I get blunt and to the point.

As the Wes turns. I know I got one life to live. At times there has to be a guiding light. When I spoke of Hollie Tucci I was being bold and telling her how beautiful she was. I'm 29 and I'm still young but I'm dealing with a lot of shit that makes me restless.

You want to know how real it is? It's too real for you to cope with. I told too many muthafuckers about the beef between my parents and me was started by them. Am I really that fuckin' crazy or do I need to repeat myself again? Sometimes I feel like I'm the only muthafuckers that knows that what really happened and how it was handled.

You ask these dumb ass questions why does a Christmas card play into me staying with Tracy. Let me break it down for you again so you'll understand.

My parents knew about what happened to Tracy and his family. The ones I told were Tony, Kenyetta, Ryan, Sonja, Angela, Antoinette, and Shay. When Tracy and his family got evicted my aunt was supposedly helping them when I got in jail.

Tracy moves to Cramer Hill and gets his own place. I don't know how my mom got Tracy's address but my mom waits until she got the first opportunity smokin' to put me on Tracy inconviently. She sends a Christmas card to Tracy and not one to his family isn't that ironic. How ironic she made the infamous I couldn't move back home quote a week after Tracy's family moved.

Not one letter. No phone call. Nothing for seven months and I had to find out through Dominic's mother. Supposedly she got his address from Tracy but really had it since last year. What supports my theory is this. I got released from jail on February 25, 2003 and Christmas is December 25th. I'm only out three hours and I got Voorhees Police Dept. in my face, I got arrested on that restraining order bullshit on March 4, 2003 but the case is mysteriously thrown out.

She supposedly got his address a few days before that restraining order bullshit but the Christmas card goes to Tracy's place 2 ½- 3 months before the case. Anybody with half a gnat's brain knows that was a set-up from the fuckin' door.

Then I had to shut these muthafuckers up at Phase One for being arrogant. I don't have any patience to play the hang-up game with a litter of dumb muthafuckers who are mad because I pissed on them. You can't play me enough to think I can't pick up who's who. I called for Harmizell about me getting published not because I wanted to rub it in.

See what happens when you try to be courteous and polite on the phone when I try to be nonchalant they want to be smart-asses. Well you can't outsmart a smart ass. I can pick up voices very well over the phone. Kenyetta and her mother are the only ones that I can't pick up.

The little visit to warn those about the disrespect will cease. That was a final warning that I'm in no mood to play the game of pin the tail on Wes. What made me catch myself was the fact that Hollie was there. Nobody told them to do another muthafuckin nigga's dirt. I knew the nigga was the mastermind behind the shit from day one. I told you that you can't play me like you think. I just played dumb.

Out of respect for Hollie, I let it slide and that will be the last time I let those muthafuckers get it off. The next hang-up, I don't care if Hollie's there then the muthafuckin' deal is off.

That wasn't trash-talking anything now is my fault. For saying Sonja Cuccu-nat-hoe now I can catch a verbal aggravated assault. Brandi Rowe can have a little stinkin' ass attitude and I'll throw her ass in the fuckin' trashcan. My bratty ass sister and I hate each other so much now and Shay's a Kahlil Jamal fan.

I'm airing out all my dirt. I don't care if I have to scream til' my lungs hurt. I'll tell you how I feel and I'm not jerkin' to porn when I said it. It may be hard to believe but I finally grew up. I'm not that goofy little teenager that went to Camden High School.

You want some shock? Well the value went down because I'm predictably unpredictable. There's a certain presence when I present that all these eyes shift in my direction that hearts stop and I'm like…

"Dag!"

Kiss Harmizell and I found that to be…well…the lip lock? I kind of liked it. Any other girl seems to thinks that I'm evil.

I'm gonna be that guy that singled out. Now I'm a cornered animal and ready to attack you like a hungry wolverine. I'm itching to scratch up a muthafuckers who antagonize me out of my character.

I can bully B-Wise so ridiculously. I don't care if you weigh 250 lbs. If you hit me that hot water and that hook off is a fuckin' retaliation. You can't hit me that hard to knock me out. It just ain't in your arsenal for you to think that you wouldn't get shitted on by Dirty.

My mind has an alter ego that can make me unlock Wicked Wes. I only go to a certain degree with Delgado. Wicked Wes is like the equal highest bar to a terror alert when America goes into a stage of emergency. Y'all sleep on Wesman like I'm entitled to you thinking that I won't give a piece of my mind. I'm that fed up with a lot of rumors and a lot of lies that are spreaded about me that ain't true. I got counters so wide that will leave Victor Newman broke.

Come one! Come all! Is that the Dirty Delgado coming out of me?

"Ah no!"

Is it about telling my side of the story?

"Yeah!"

I had a date for Dominic's wedding and I wound up standing Angela up. Thanks to my fuckin' mom and that damn restraining order. I'm totally annoyed by that. She knows what she did and now she's a victim of circumstance? Yeah alright keep believing that!

You can think I went psychotic I have my reasons for being driven crazy. I don't have a record of a DWI. As badly I want to fuck motherfuckers up I want to kill a Haitian bitch. I got to remember if I do that I'll get a whole lot of prison time and I'm not built for that.

I'd rather throw salt in the wounds. It saves me a case. If I'm calling women bitches then you must've did something really fucked up because I would never come out my mouth sideways to be speaking like that. You can hurt muthafuckers up by using words than you could by punching them in the face.

I speak…I speak…I speak. I'm a grown ass man. I got grown up problems. I got grown up problems with grown up idiots with grown ups that do childish shit that a kindergartner would do. The bar for me to fail in this book is extremely high. I can't disappoint the public and prove these jokers wrong. I'm not a one-time wonder and I keep that title "The World's Greatest Writer."

I start a project, I got the swagger. If I go snapping and sniping then I'm Wes Allen Muhammad. I won't kill you just see me in the book. I won't say shit I'll give myself a reason to go on the attack. You must've done something to piss me off. Why would I have a reason?

By the jeers I get you could've swore I was a basketball player who's been accused of raping a white girl. By me being sweet and normal I saw the arrogance of ignorance in people that I never did shit to. Fuck that shit, you don't start know shifty shit then I won't polk fun of you.

Don't ever feel like I lost my head. Nothing hasn't changed the way the public views me. From being called annoying to being in trouble for hooking bus drivers. You can run and tell A.D that Wes said that his mom can really suck my little dick. If you try to play me out I'll spit on you like I spit on him.

I have been on my best behavior to those who don't believe me. I keep telling people that I'm not the bad guy in this shit. Now that I been stained as one I got sick of trying to change the views I have no control over. Fuck it now I found out I need to do shit that will put a smile on my face again.

If I gave Hollie Tucci teddy bears out of kindness I can get an "Awwwwww" one minute and then get negative feedback the next. There just have to be a way for muthafuckers to find a reason to give me a black eye so I can get passed over for humanitarian of the year award. It ain't no different how it was with Shay six years ago.

I even lose jobs over making an effort to at least trying to get to work. You think drinking out of coffee mugs was a stupid ass excuse try walking down Route 130 from Willingboro to Delran and you'll feel what I'm saying. On top of that I' broke as shit.

If it was worth Al Valentine's good guy image to have somebody fat to cover up his shit then I should've never bought the girl a new damn mug. That teddy bear I bought was a waste of fuckin' money too. I say fuck it give it to the girl you care about the most for being sneaky and stealing your job.

They call me crazy because I explained my feelings for how I felt about a Tucci. Now let Marianne call those damn Pegans to come and shoot me.

"Ooops! I said it!"

You really think I give a fuck about my desire to retract shit I say and it ain't about to get attention it's about America in general. I don't any slept rocks getting shit all twisted up. You can say this is the chapter I was itching to go off. Relieving some attention and saying it in rhythm. I feel about 50,011 times worse.

My life is fucked up. Fuck it! Fuck the world's view of me. Fuck the opinions. Fuck Guerdy Baguidy. Fuck Voorhees Police. Fuck my mom and that weak ass restraining order. Fuck if people read me going off. Fuck it if they think I need help.

Fuck a lot of shit. Fuck liking a rich girl I'd rather stay ghetto and broke. Fuck my brat of a sister. Fuck whoever else doesn't like what I write. I got felony convictions and I admit what I did last year was a mistake. My parents don't love me and my mom likes seeing me in jail. The fuckin' hypocrite.

If you read me from Lisa Perkins to my nigga Ruben Forzani then you knew I really did care for Hollie Tucci.

"Here's the shit in writing so tell people more shit about
me that already isn't a secret in Voorhees."

To the Stage

(CHAPTER TWENTY-ONE)

Here we go! Here we go!

To the stage!

Here we go! Here we go!

To the stage!

Here we go! Here we go!

To the stage

Here we go! Here we go!

The Wesman had to compose all the negative showoffs that tried to outshine me knowing that they can't and that I'm blessed with all that intelligence to know how to get my voice heard. It seems like it was so long ago that I came out with a new piece and I haven't been the center of attention for a while. This is a totally different muthafucker that you're witnessing that's more mature and only speaking on his terms.

I didn't respond back to a lot of the shit I was hearing because I came out with that last piece of work when I needed some much needed R&R. Well now that I'm relaxed and ready to introduce myself to the world my throne is the hotseat. If you thought I was gonna burn than you must be gravely mistaken. If I'm on the hotseat I'm throwing you under the bus.

That's right the Wes Daddy Mack is kicking ass and naming names in the process. I'm cutting the check. From what I remember there was only one sheriff in town and his name is Dirty Delgado. You ran out of your cards and I'm still playing with my deck if I'm not killing people for fun then I must be toying with new suicide bomb experiments.

It's lights, camera, action and what you might've done is thrown out the window because all eyes are on me and you're just lost in the mix. Yeah I got my issues but they must be that intriguing for you to be caught up in it. I'm back at it once again and I'm looking for that encore that I bring in every book that I write.

They say that you're only as good as your last book and I don't see it that way. I keep it popping because you know I might say the unpredictable and I may not make sense to you even if I say it because I leave you out in the dark and I may not shed light in what the meeting is behind it. It makes sense to me because my job is to have you keep guessing about what I may do for my next act.

I feel that flow when I get fluent when I get down on the microsoft and bust out some words when I'm putting out a chapter. I'm only doing this off the top of my head and I don't need a yellow legal pad I'm not hungry enough to do that anymore.

You feel like you had the need to address me and I feel like you had enough of your say. Well it's time to fire back the only way Wes knows how. I do it by....

"Taking it to the Stage!"

I'm tired of hearing shit that I slept with somebody's sister. I'm tired of hearing shit that I'm alledgedly gay because I don't have a girlfriend. I'm tired of hearing lies why I'm mysteriously attacking muthafuckers. I'm tired of hearing shit and getting the character getting confused from the man. I have the microphone in my hand and it's my turn to speak on it.

It seems pretty intriguing that when my name is in it that shit seems to get twisted or that the truth is being told to a degree and that niggas know the story and my side still haven't been spoken. Then when I say or shall I say speak then the truth is spoken then the one that mixed up the truth is fumbling over their words.

They don't want me to speak because they want you to know and what they don't want you to know. I get the criticism from all sort of angles that they want to be the one that wants to take me out and it hasn't been proven and I like to see if you have what it takes to go against me when we go in a heated debate.

You best believe that you're haunted and I'm something like the curse of the Bambino. It won't take 86 years for it to be lifted and I'm in no mood to reverse it but I want to agitate it and antagonize it til' I get pretty bored. Look at those that try to burn me and how that person has gone downhill and how I rise above them.

I don't really need to harbor feelings when you're still stewing about what I did to comeback well you tried to reach my soul and you only called check. I play for checkmate and I tell you that checkers and chess are two different ballgames.

You think that we're still playing checkers well that's one game I hate to play since I learned how to play chess in the ninth grade. I play you into a trap and I want you to get into it and I'm up for a challenger and I'm more than inviting you to go against me. You know that you're going against a juggernaut and I'm the wrong one for you to be calling out but you put your head on the chopping block and I just was willing to serve you on a platter.

If I call you out you best believe there's a reason. It's a response behind the action of the instigator. You got me going there for a minute until I decide that I need to have my run of fun.

If you need to address me and you want to be sly about it then I know how to take it. I take it to a stage that you don't want me to take it and I proven to y'all that you're dealing with the mystique and it's a tough hill to conquer. A wolverine knows how to attack and this one picks his fights on his terms.

My name has been called out once again even when I was taking a break. Welcome to the circus and we have the clowns, jugglers, the trapeze, and my life is under the big top. I've been smelling blood on you before my chapter hits the fan. The World's Greatest Writer is about to start some shit.

Your former co-workers and your peers know that you ain't got nothing for Wesman. You're just trying to put up a brave face but you know that you pretty much got defeated. You said you want it with me well you haven't shown me that you peaked my curiousity. While I'm all souped up and fired up there's some bitches running around claiming that I had sex with her sister spreading lies because she wants to say her sister fucked a nigger.

I only know how to cause so much chaos. I'm out to start a buzz and it doesn't involve me running around naked killing people with a chainsaw. I'm at it again and knocking you out the park like Barry Bonds sends it to McCovey Cove. Call your bosses, your c/o's, Ancora, Voorhees Police if you want I'll just tell them that I verbally killed you and be arrogant about how I did it.

It's been a while well I'm here and still that tongue is sharper than a swinging guillotine and it's more lethal, because you think because I matured now that my words would be more mellow. I need a little drama so why don't you swing some my way but it's too risky to try. It's not like you were warned that coming in this direction was the worng way to turn because they told you that nigga Wesman is a name that can make you go nuts and drive you crazy. The girls shake their heads and they know who was the nigga that did it.

I mean you want to take it up with me. Maybe you're too stupid to recognize that I have everything to gain and nothing to lose from the standpoint I'm looking at. I'm out to fight and it doesn't matter who wants to be the next victim.

They tell you don't listen to me because I supposedly lost my damn mind. Well...yeah I lost it and it seems right that I hit the computer like I'm slapping a bitch around to have another restraining order filed on me. Writing shit that has me under indictment and the names that has me bragging about how I did it and got away with it.

It's amazing how I was hated and how they continued to read me. It seems like ages ago when my name was too wicked for a conversation and now I get more respect based off the fact that I carried so much on my plate like Jesus was when he was being mocked when he carried that cross to Nazareth.

It sounds like something that would come out of me. That ain't nothing new when you read a guy like me. Then again they haven't been able to comprehend a guy of the likes of Kahlil Weston and that's the crazy part. They like it when I have something interesting to say because that's the power of my personality speaks because it's that's strong and I ain't hungry to kill names and watch them burn after I through it around like your Raggedy Ann.

If I was a girl with a long nose and I was green I would be the wicked witch. Well I was born with a scrotum and I can break you down with just one of many ways. If you think that you know my weaknesses and they're not open well you got to find it and I won't disclose them to you. I may be in the mood to start up and that what makes the plot thicken because I leave you in suspense.

To all my friends and this goes out to all those who want to know when I wrtie and what I'm all about. Let's take this back to Voorhees Township, I may have been raised in Camden, yeah I needed to set records straight and these are rebuttals. Yes I do accept that dispute that I'm that I'm pretty controversial and that I play both sides of the fences.

Muthafuckers need to stop and understand that this ain't child's play. It just came to me that something is on my mind and that I want to share what I think. I may want you to take me serious as I have a goal. I have a lot to speak on and the situation is sure looking sticky. It's not that gross like Cameron Diaz got some gel confused for something else like she did on "There's Something About Mary".

Well I tell you "There's Something About Kahlil". I'm simple enough to talk about my issues and put em' down like there's nothing to it. I got you caught up into my own little world and I have to admit that I'm pretty flattered that you would think that way.

Your best bet if you don't want to be put out there because if you feel like you have some shit on me believe me you don't. I'll hang your ass out to dry and you'll be contradicting yourself like you'll wish you never started some shit. My business is already out there and it's like so what we already know that so it ain't something shattering or groundbreaking that will rattle me. Because my business was already out there and yours ain't and I expose it, I'm like a celeb who had a fuckin' groupie and this nigga will tell you about the shit you do.

You could see that my demeanor is more serious then it's ever been and that I can make myself the nightmare you'll never wake up from. I just want to blast somebody like Ray Lewis blew up Laverneus Coles. That's the the type of shit I'm into. I got all this built up inside of me and it was itching for me come out and they say you can't take the fight out the fighter.

I still feel that fire that I need to get it off me or I'll fuckin' explode like a deadly combination of a match mixed with nitrogen. My mouth is too foul for me to be chewing into a bar of soap. Better yet I'm just the bad apple that spit in the face of people that don't want to be cool. I feel that mean streak in me.

You don't like me well you know that it's a fuck you with a purpose and I can be direct if you want me to say it to your face. I might've went through an evolution but I'm still Muhammd Ali when he was proclaiming himself a bad man. You can get the band ready because I'm feeling pretty sadistic.

You know that all hell has just broken loose and I'm out of jail. Come on niggas you know that Wes is real cute. I know you bitches that call me out and bad mouth me, I know you want to say you got your shit off on my expense. Then when I talked so much shit about you back in your face it's like a humbling, humiliation, and I can have witnesses testify to that.

I'm still kicking ass and taking names in the process and it seems like that your checkbook is running low and I got that mouth running and I'm still disrespecting muthafucker at a drop of dime. I want it to be something for you to remember me by. Nobody wants to see me when I'm on top of my game.

You want to get it on and I'm welcomed to the idea. Better yet I'm game and it's bad news for those to know that I'm back and better than I was when you saw me with a broken spirit. I had to join alliances with an old friend that was watching from afar. When the word was spreading that I was gonna be a force to be reckoned with and it spelled trouble the roaches ran for cover because they didn't want to kick me anymore now that I wasn't down anymore.

I came back for so many reasons because it's time to spark that buzz. It's time for you to witness mystique when you see it. Seeing a man like me typing is like a masterpiece and believe me I'll take you to school. I've taken enough muthafuckers that I need to be a principal and you can bring me an apple after I shitted all over you like it was child's play.

I might've gone too Hollywood once too many. I'm friends with a cheerleader and it's sort of like now I'm hot again. It's like I had to smooth out my image and now I'm getting the overdue respect, I'm not into making ammence with those that had me written off. I got a trick under my sleeve and you couldn't imagine what I got in that bag.

Well that's the beauty of knowing me because I keep you in the dark. When I want to display what I've done it's like black magic and a bunch of hocus pocus. I don't don a black top hat but I can pull a rabbit out of it. I've done it before and don't think I can't do it again.

I think it doesn't dawn on muthafuckers who I am and what I can do. I've done it before and so help me I'll prove you wrong again. Just one more time do I have to address another set of issues in my book. Just one more book I'll write before I hang it up. Just one more time must I find a way to piss the world off with the shit I say.

There's a whole bunch of grown-ups that act like kids and tell those who are curious to know what you got to say. I got grown-ups snatching shit from grown-ups about me and my book and what I speak. If you tell them don't read me they'll do it behind your back anyway so how are you gonna stop them.

This goes out to those who want the latest 4-1-1 you can't dial (856)308-2731 if you want to talk all this shit about me. I had to change my number so you can't threaten me or say I'm a real man and run your mouth. I'm the World's Greatest Writer and I speak on my own terms. I did talk shit and respond the only way I know how and that's starting a war of words.

In my own little world the beef really starts when I speak and not when the challenger draws first blood but I get the last laugh. When I'm done dragging you through the mud then I may consider it over and as of right now I only began to fight and it makes you fume that I had niggas taking my side and not yours.

I draw you into my own little spiderweb and you're tangled up. You're so caught up that the opinion you had before my rebuttal no longer exist they want to talk about me. You're so screwed that I have to get my mouth running, and whip you with an extension cord. I hear the ooohhs and aaahhs from an earshot away.

When it's on the stage I should feel right at home and it's like I go without further adieu and I know that there's a lot of muthafuckers who want to say break a leg but in a negative way and I'm not trying to do that. I have to take a bow and deliver the performance. It's lights, camera, action! I see that spotlight shining on me and it's just where I want it to be.

I'm right at home when I'm up on the stage. One thing you learn is that when I want the spotlight I don't want a co-star. I don't need an Oscar to put on an award winning performance. I got the jokes to prove it. I'm the franchise for a reason and I can carry a book by myself. Putting a book out and taking the spotlight is when I throw my weight in the ring and there ain't a fuckin thing you can do to stop it.

Face it you can't kill Kahlil. Then there's no doubt who's #1now. I tell you this there is a challenge I would like to know who would like to go at it with next. If you want to know who I would like to lock horns with find out when I write the cliffhanger in the final chapter.

Terroristic Negotiations

(CHAPTER TWENTY TWO)

The President: That's rights...lick it right there. Oh like that. I like the top of job you do when you blow. I feel the milk coming on. Let me get the shake to fly out.....

(The Phone Rings)

The President: Keep going I can talk and you can blow. (Picks up the phone) Hello Oval Office.

"Dirty": I got your fuckin country in a state of emergency and that's all you think about is making decisions with your pants down and she's blowing you with her favorite blouse on.

The President: Well! Well! Well! If it ain't "Dirty" bin Laden. I guess you feel right at home doing your act of terrorism. You won't get away with this.

"Dirty": I've been getting' away with shit since 1993 when I tried to blow up those damn buildings. I took all those souls to visit the devil. I had those pilots do that in love for Allah.

The President: You were willing to tear families apart forever by doing that vicious blatant act by taking four airplanes around the U.S. and purposely take lives of those who did nothing to you.

"Dirty": I thought it was pretty funny. I never realized how easy it was to hijack an airplane. It's kind of equivalent to robbing a bank don't you think. You Americans do not have respect for Allah. If you learned how to run your country and stop cheating on your wife you could've stopped this but you didn't.

The President: It's people like you that makes this world…Stop Monica I'm conducting business…

Monica (breathing heavily after taking the dick out her mouth): O.K Mr. President.

The President: I didn't find what you did to be the least bit funny. None of those people can replace their lives that you took.

Dirty: I had a couple of my Al-Queda forces that wanted to see Dr. Kevorkian because they wanted to kill themselves and I told them how would you like to kill yourself and help me get America back at the same time.

The President: Your act of terrorism will bring you to justice. I find your plan was to get us back for the way we run our business. Our country is strong and we will not fear you.

"Dirty: You really think that the game ends there? Four planes we hijacked and two building crash we tale out a defense in D.C. and we would've had the retreat if the passengers didn't try to play tough..

The President: They were being heroes. While you guys were trying to be cowards because you did it under our noses and we think Sadaam had a hand in it. You think that's gonna stop us from doing what we do in everyday life.

"Dirty": Before I was rudely interrupted look how we saw the people run. We sell you the porn tapes from the quickie mart and we took out half of your economy. How's Wall Street gonna stay balanced? You got Gates to think for that. I bet if I was an angry white guy who wanted to take out 168 mutha fuckers in Oklahoma I wouldn't be under attack like this.

The President: We sent him t hell we gave him poison. You took peoples lives and you took out some of the police we had and they put their lives on the line to save others. You had no regard or remorse for what happened on the eleventh so don't think this will be forgotten.

"Dirty": We took actions on the eleventh but what does it represent. My porn collection is higher than the twin towers you have standing. You attacked the Middle East back in 1991. That's why the nines were flipped to eleven. Your twin tower buildings standing up look like the number eleven.

The President: So this all just a big numbers game to you. We almost ran in fear from you and you want to play war games get your country into this and you want to play coward. We got the service on alert and we're coming over to hunt you down. Don't think we're gonna sit there and let you get away with it.

"Dirty": All I got to do is stay Muslim and hide in the caves. Try to play my game my favorite is hide and go seek and I feel like playing the hunted. We hunted down our targets and we got you guessing what our next move may be.

The President: Let me tell you something "Dirty" you may lost the name Delgado but the name you have will let you know that you're the world's most wanted man. We're not running out of targets you are. We'll take out the babies who will grow up to be villains like you. We'll take you guys down if it means we hunt you to the end of the earth.

"Dirty": You talk a good one but I bet you can't hold your own in bed. Just to downgrade you if I got your wife to cheat on you and I got her pregnant you would have a stepchild who would be a junior terrorist. Bring her over here so I can knock her up and get pregnant.

The President: Now that's a low blow and I think you underestimate how strong we are in the darkest hours. The babies you made will never grow to be terrorist if we see terror in their eyes as infants one time then they'll die too.

"Dirty": You know my A.K.A and my wives but how many wives did I get pregnant. I may have one, I may have three, I may have nine or I may have three hundred. So if you kill one that doesn't mean shit to me. I guess I would be considered in your country a what you call a playboy. They say bitches ain't shit but hoes and tricks.

The President: Now you want to adopt our language? It doesn't fly like "Dirty". The red, white, and blue are as strong as it is now then it was then. This attack is worst than the assassination of Kennedy. A gunshot took that man's life but you unexpectedly took last breaths without a regard to it.

"Dirty": I consider my attack valid. Just like "A Queen and his Sidekick" was the perfect retaliation for those who decide to cross "Dirty". I move very quickly and I do my revenge in silence. This was bigger than dropping sugar down a guard's tank. Calling a team leader fat and putting her in tears. This has to be the cherry on top. I knocked down two buildings in one day.

The President: This is how you like to pay us back. You want to do Sadaam's dirty work and he doesn't give a damn about nobody except himself. We want you to bought to justice. Don't think we don't have tabs on you and G.I.'s to spy.

"Dirty": Like I'm shaking. We already have one hostage and he's a Wall Street reporter. Look how we have one of your own fighting for the Taliban. He was with us all the way. We have your country surrounded like we you don't know that you're on notice.

The President: We know your weakness "Dirty", all we have to do is bring porn stars to your cave they fuck you good and it will make you weak. We know about the people you killed out in Voorhees and the unsolved case of the male hooker that came up missing so don't think we have FBI file on you.

"Dirty": That doesn't mean shit. All it means to me is that I did the other fugitives in America a favor because they're not looking for them. I'm the man that you got to catch. Where can I be? In the cave? The private jet? In the back of someone's car with a machete set to swing? You got kill me to find me.

The President: Now you're telling me that it's hard to find you. It ain't hard to know your whereabouts. Don't think you're untouchable because you're not. You got the war with the Israelis so we're not the only ones you have problems with.

"Dirty": You better worry about your country and stop worrying about them. We got you guys running for fear. Do you really hold my clan responsible for a plane flying into the Brooklyn-Queens Bridge it looks like America needs to sleep with one eye open.

The President: I wouldn't put anything by you dirty terrorist. Dirty is right up your alley. You might have put Voorhees in fear but you won't do that to the America.

"Dirty": We're nothing like the people in Iraq. We helped Iraq take over Kuwait all those years ago. You want to stick your noses in our takeover. We wanted to make more money by taking over the oil those bastards have on their soil but you had to come and spoil the fun.

The President: I can concentrate on taking you guys out and I can have my pants up when I do it. You really think you're funny and you did it without a clear conscience.

"Dirty": Maybe I did it because you wouldn't let me bang up Jenna Jameson. I want to run the economy of your nation by starting a stock spree in porn. I needed to take out trade central with a blink of an eye. I didn't expect that much damage done but I consider what I had my troopers do was a deed for me. David Koesch would've been proud.

The President: Listen up "Dirty" we now know what you're capable of doing. You may be the villain of the year and you consider the act of terrorism black humor.

"Dirty": I had to teach you to see "Dirty" bin Laden's way and if you don't do what I say that reporter won't be alive for that much longer. We got his wife wondering what we'll to her husband. He may not get to see his unborn child and we want to set an example that we're not playing. We'll shoot him in the head and send his body back to America with a ribbon and bow attached.

The President: What the hell do you mean by what you just said. He's just an innocent man and you want to take his life. I guess it makes you feel good to kill Americans in cold blood. If we got to smoke you out with gas bombs we will. If you want to mess with the big boys we got the Marines on the way and we'll see how you measure up to them.

"Dirty": This wasn't a joke when 9:03 am was on that date. I saw Katie Couric in a short skirt and I wanted her to be notice who did it. We hit the towers eighteen minutes apart and before you recover we hit the Pentagon. We were really pist off because we wanted Gore to win Florida. Have you forgot the secret deal that you and I had?

The President: What secret deal?

"Dirty": Oh! Now you don't know shit. What the fuck you think this is. You think I didn't forget about the threesome I was suppose to have with your daughters. I don't play when it comes to deal I will do you foul to get my point across. When I play dirty I play within the rules.

The President: Well the rule you played said you wanted it with us. We don't forget who tries to shit on us. You bastards think it's a game but it's not. You got a nation to take on and you don't come to American soil and get us running.

"Dirty": Like Public Enemy once said…"It takes a nation of millions to hold us back." How far can you go to bring us to justice? I got the resources to get a nuclear bomb and get the radiation started from D.C. to Canada. We'll shit on a country like we took laxative.

The President: Let me tell you something "Dirty" bin Laden. You should call off any other plans before we put it on you.

"Dirty": The fun has already begun. Where will we strike next? You got to find out what we're up to. It's up for us to execute and you to find out. We shut down your operation so bad we made cell phones shut down. I'm proud of those who sacrificed their lives to see you muthafuckers get what should've came to you eleven years ago.

The President: You better give us Dan back or there will be dire consequences.

"Dirty": We don't give a fuck. We'll use him as a human shield in one of the caves. If you want to make a catch and throw us in jail its not gonna happen. You have to kill us. You're at war alright and we didn't come to play games.

The President: it doesn't work like that if you mess with innocent people you take on the whole nation. If you didn't want it you were better off not saying shit and just stay in the Middle East but you came to our land and spit on our soil. You taking shots at those people was like you taking shots at me.

"Dirty": Now you sound like that old fossil Chuck Fakeley. We want it we don't think you have the pussy to come out here and challenge us. The leaders won't tell you where I am because I paid them off. I give them money and they won't snitch. They may act like they want to help but they work for me.

The President: Listen up well. We told them that we wanted you and turn you over to us. You're facing a lawsuit and other types of people who will hunt you down for coming at us sideways.

"Dirty": You ain't see nothing yet and you didn't hear the last of us. We made the streets in the Arab world celebrate in joy. We don't feel any pain because my followers have Allah on our side. Just when you feel me, I can be in Pakistan. I like to keep you at bay so you can wonder what I'm up to next.

The President: Don't think for a minute we're gonna let you run over us. We'll cut off your bank supplies so we can find out how are you gonna survive.

"Dirty": Fuck this shit I'm tired of hearing you talk a lot of shit I think I need to show you what type of actions. I'll get my second in charge to bring over the hostage in our custody. Now give us another plane to crash into another building or we kill him on the spot.

The President: We'll send you a handful of porn tapes if you set him free. It doesn't have to be that way. Just hand him over to us and this can be easily fixed.

"Dirty": I don't feel like you Americans can keep your word. You have a congressman who killed an intern and you never charged him. Why should we believe you? Yo Rubeno?

Ruben: What up dogs?

"Dirty": Bring him over here. I think it's time for him to meet his maker. Remember the picture we showed with the gun to his head. I really think we should kill him now and send a strand of his hair to let em know that we touched a hair on his head.

The President: bin Laden don't do it. You made your point if you do it now we're gonna send them to attack just turn yourself over and nobody has to be hurt. You and the rest of your clan.

"Dirty": I want it with y'all puny Americans. Give the gun to put the bullet in his brain and see it fall like JFK's did. We're gonna set the example that we came to fight and we got more in store.

The President: Stop it ain't worth it. You son of a bitch don't kill that man he's about to start a family.

"Dirty": Ruben take the phone so I can take his life. He has the blindfold to his head and he doesn't know when his life will be taken so let's just do him let him hear the cry of the gun that puts him in heaven with the angels.

The President: bin Laden don't do it. It just ain't right for this man to die…..

"Dirty": Die in the honor of Allah. And may flights of angels send thee to thy rest

(Sounds of the gun shot)

Bang! Bang!….Bang! Bang!

"Dirty": Heh! Heh! Heh! Heh! Heh!

PAID OFF PLAYER
(SKIT)

Wes: Goddamn this girl is thorough!

Ruben: She's healthy but you don't get pussy Wes.

Wes: You crazy as hell you never seen the Wesman at work.

Ruben: I got ten dollars saying that you won't get that tricks phone number.

Wes: Run that!

(Walking over)

Wes: Excuse me!

Girl: Yes! Hey! Aren't you Wes Daddy Mack?

Wes: That be me!

Girl: You know Nancy Haash she told me you were really cute but I had know idea you were that fine. She's not lying when she called you a cutie.

Wes: It's nice to find an admirer but I have to admit I had an ulterior motive to come over and get to know some of my endearing fans.

Girl: Oh really?

Wes: Yeah! While I was eyeing you from the other side of the room you caught my eye. You see I bet my boy Ruben ten dollars that I get your phone number.

Girl: That light skin guy with the Afro. Is he black?

Wes: He's Dominican!

Girl: Oh really!

Wes: Mm-hmm!

Girl: Here's ten dollars. Go pay your friend and tell him I like to talk to him.

Wes (talking in his mind): Bitch!

(walking back over)

Ruben: And? What happened?

Wes: She gave me ten dollars to pay you and that she wanted to talk to you instead.

Ruben: Watch my work and see how I pull this little trick. Give me my loot nigga.

Wes: Fuck you Ruben! You may get the bitch but I'm keeping the ten dollars.

Any Questions (Part I)

(CHAPTER TWENTY-FIVE)

So now that your is out what do you for a second act?

I plan on bringing out quite a plenty before I decide to drop the pen. There's gonna be a series of books coming out I have the titles done for a few and there are some I did but I lost the material to them so I have to come up with new ideas.

So what is The Kahlil Weston Hour about?

This one is a little more personal for me in so many ways. It's to let y'all know this is Kahlil Weston. I'm still the same crazy, wild and a joker but I'm still me. I have a more personal stake and I'll get deeper if you continue to follow my writing.

When will you work on the second one?

It may be done you just to see when it hits the print.

Do you have plans on doing a third?

Heh! Heh! Heh! You'll just have to wait and see.

You bought up something that raised eyebrows. You said men have a feminine side. Why do you think that?

When I said that heads turn. If men didn't have a feminine side he wouldn't know how to love. A lot of men won't admit that because they have an image to protect. Just because you have that side doesn't mean you're gay.

Kahlil Weston

What brings out feminism in a man?

His sensitive and caring side. He's not afraid to express his feelings. He comes down to a vulnerable level and he's down to earth. He becomes a sweet individual.

Does it work around women in your eye?

It does. It impresses a lot people when I bring that up. Everytime I bring that up a lot of women agree with me. It surprises people when I go from acting crazy to down to earth.

You're portrayed as a bad person and you seem like a nice kid. Some of the words have you pegged as darker to the core. Do you think you have a bad rap?

It really doesn't make a difference to me. Of course people that can't stand me will see me as the bad guy. They act like they're good guys but it makes their image look cheesy. I grab the image and the popularity and they take a back seat.

Do you worry about what people think about you?

No! Back when I was younger I did. I'm my own person. If I worry about trying to convince the world that I'm not a bad person then I'm wasting my time.

When people talk about you how does it make you feel?

Actually I'm flattered whether it's positive or negative. I must be doing something right to get that attention. Somebody has to show the balls and I did. If I cause controversy then I know the reaction will be mixed. I already know what I'm doing this stuff I just see how many jaws drop.

Is it a must for you to fire off at adversaries?

Whoa! I'm just pulling their cards. Those who act like I'm the bad guy need to be told about themselves. Here's an example I bash Haitian women but not the males.

You took shots in all directions what angles are you trying to come from. Do you feel like Kahlil takes pride in poking fun at people?

That's not Kahlil doing that.

You must be talking about your alter ego Dirty Delgado. Who is he?

Dirty Delgado is Kahlil Weston's best friend. He protects Kahlil from harm. He comes out when he needs to. The Wes Daddy Mack may be my moniker but Dirty Delgado is a muthafucker. When he comes out he's out to do damage.

Is that you blowing the kiss of revenge?

You can say that. I use my insults and shoot my enemies down like wounded duck. I just fire off and they need to learn Dirty Delgado isn't Kahlil Weston.

You have been called mentally disturbed for acts you done. They read and they really think you gone crazy. Do you rub people the wrong way? You're developing a reputation.

You're telling me something that I already know about. Whether I'm good or not I'm gonna rub people the wrong way. All I can do is be me. If you don't like the shit I do then don't read me.

Do you think bad boys are good guys?

I'm not a bad boy I do bad things.

O.k. do you like the image you portray? Being Kahlil…do you feel like you changed?

I'm still Wes! This is me. Just because I write books don't think of me any different just treat me normal. I'm still the same Kahlil that raises hell in his book. I'm the foul-mouthed s.o.b that likes to talk shit. If I try to be someone I'm not then you're robbing me of me. I'll be unhappy when you try to put that noose around me. It's still all about Wes and not about you.

Are you doing this for attention or are you putting on an act?

Maybe I am and maybe I'm not. It ain't my fault you're caught up in what I do. Not just you but other people. If I know I did some thing that drew attention…I just wait for that reaction that makes you say "oh shi"…

We get the message do feel like you have to go out and prove something? You dog people out when you use your alter-ego doing that proves that you create a hostile image.

Hmmm! I dog people out. I might dog them out because they tried they're damnest to dog me out and they may be the one with the problem. Hippocrits that try to act like they're innocent. They weren't goody goody when they were doing they're dirt. They give me the act and they can't follow their own advice. They wanna dish it out but can't take it.

Critics claim that you have a big mouth.

Yeah! Yeah! They call me crazy too. Now they wonder why I took shots at the good ol' Rev. Eugene.

Why did you take shot at him the way you did?

He bought his shit the day he decided to keep fuckin' with me and he needed to learn that I'm not the one to mess with. He acts like he's a loving person but I find him nauseatingly empty. He likes to choke women. He was always on a smear Wes campaign. I guess I became so popular it didn't sit well with him and he felt left out in the cold. It goes to show how far you get in life if you do hippocrit type of shit.

You feel like he was jealous of you?

Wes knows he was. I can accomplish more by accident than he did by trying.

You think he's a good reverend?

Personally think he's garbage. He needs to be growing a perm like Al Sharpton.

You take a lot of heat. You seem to handle it pretty well. Are you concerned with possible lawsuits when you verbally attack?

Not really I've been kicked out of college and been through the N.J. State Prison system. I've been through worse. If Christie wants to fine me I'll make sure I put it on my income tax form. He's pretty much taxing me for mouthing off. Now I'm being told how I can and can't use my mouth. That's like robbing me of freedom of speech. They can say my book suck that's cool. If it sucked that bad then you paid for a book that you claimed suck. It was still good enough for you to put money in my back pocket.

Let's get animated…if you died and came back as a woman who would you be.

Chante' Moore!

Why her?

I love her facial structure. What I really love is her feminism, her whole feature. Hearing her sing is like my writing it's hypnotizing.

You ever thought about being a politician? You have a lot of issues.

No! If I did I'll break every law known to man. I'll be the politician that slept with the intern. If I was the governor of New Jersey the first thing I would do is kick Christie out the damn state.

Would you actually have sex with a porn star?

Put a wild turkey in my hand, get me drunk, get Lana Sands naked and she makes out with that female lawyer who's a pornstar and anything is libel to happen.

Would you do a porno movie?

If I did I would put a bag over my head.

Who would star in your porno movie?

I'm hitting Serenity raw dog.

You're not right.

I like being wrong…well accused wrong.

There some good girls in the church give them a try.

Yeah! Well…if I did then I can't do bad things. I sure as hell can't follow the Ten Commandments. I still haven't gotten fornicating and adultery out of my system.

Do you have a girlfriend?

No!

Does it bother you?

It did when I was younger. There's nothing wrong living the single life but I really want a real relationship. I'm in no rush to be in a relationship like I was in the past. When the time comes to take it serious I'll know just for today I have to live with being a bachelor.

You pretty much sounded off in your book do you feel threatened by them in anyway? I see how you went off in certain chapters.

My mouth was gunning to shoot off for a minute. I had to show them it's not Kahlil vs. them…they get Dirty Delgado. I like talking trash I feel like if your mama is ugly then you need to be told the truth. Personally…I don't think there's too many people that can go word for word with me.

What's your concept of talking trash?

Just to get in somebody's head. I play around with your mind. If somebody wants to say something smart God gave me a mouth to talk shit. I use trash talking as a motivation. It gives me reasons to beat you.

How did the trash talking start?

When I was 16. Over the years I developed it as a craft. It reached a point I go on and on. I just use it talk you out of your game and then be cocky about it. It feels good to talk trash and you win.

I have to ask you about your lovelife. You make no secret that the girl you like is white. You caught a lot of heat for that. How do you handle it?

I don't feel any pressure liking her. It's not the prejudice it's the fear of the prejudice. Whether I was black or white I'm still a human being. I'm entitled to have feelings too. If I was white it would've never been a big deal but because I was black I had to wear it.

Kahlil Weston

Could you settle down and actually hold a relationship?

You may not believe it but I actually can.

I heard a rumor that you're dedicating the book to Hollie Tucci is that true?

I really had no idea that I was gonna dedicate it to Hollie but the rumor was true. I called her and told her that the original stuff was almost done and she would get the original stuff I wrote. She asked me and I was like well yeah. She's the one I cared about so it only seemed fair. I can say how much I like this chick or that chick but I know who I like. So I might as well say she's number one but I come before anybody. I doubt it now.

Who is the woman you lovethe most?

Shay!

Rumors are flying that Shay may company as far as who do you love. What's going on with that?

Next Question!

Are you afraid of getting your feelings hurt?

Nah! Been there...done that! It just seems less painful because I been shot down so many times. I talk to girls with expectations very low. I took a look in the mirror, it may not be me it might be them. If they feel like they can do better then enough power to them. That's their lack of vision.

How would you like to fall in love?

I like to be caught off guard. It starts off as friends and all of a sudden the friendship goes to another level. I want to fall in love because I felt it in me. I don't want to fall in love because I was forced to.

Do you think that's the type of love Kahlil wants?

I can't ask or force a girl to fall in love with me. She has to feel it for herself....flip it!

That's why a lot of relationships are dysfunctional. They fall in love for the wrong reasons. They get treated like trash and they stay. People get caught up in that image shit and it shouldn't be about that. If that person treats you like shit and takes you for granted then leave em'. Your happiness comes before anything. A lot of people put their eggs in one basket. They never save a little for themsleves. I guess it's the fear of being lonely. The only girl I was with seriously was Shay and she took me for granted as far as Guerdy was concerned she turned out to be a fuckin' bitch. Sometimes you have to take a step back and say is this person gonna treat me right. They force themselves to fall in love and they don't study or analyze the person.

Do you feel like it was fate that made your attraction to Hollie natural?

I had no control over what I was feeling for Hollie.

Who would you consider a role model on how to treat a woman?

Daniel Petite!

Who is he?

He's Antoinette Ragone's husband. I see how those two love each other and I wish I could do that with Hollie but I can't make her or force Hollie to do it. I see how those two display their affection for one another and they don't fight a lot. I remember when I paid for Antoinette's drink and he didn't get jealous. When I bought Antoinette a plush lamb and I told her Dan better not come after me with a loaded shotgun. She said Dan knows me and he'll say…"Oh that's from Kahlil…I know who he likes."

Did Kahlil Weston fall in love?

Angela thinks I did and Tracy thinks I did. If I did I know I did it for all the right reasons because I cared for Hollie very much. Hollie brings shit out of me that I never felt. It's a feeling that I can't explain it make me feel full.

The answer Wes did Kahlil Weston fall in love?

I don't know I just don't know.

Transmitting the Message

(Chapter Twenty-Five)

Back on 9/11, I heard a voice. I heard it I telepathically made out the translation it was from bin Laden. He told me about the issues that he had with America. He told me about the shit he thought that McVeigh did was pretty cool, so he told me about a plot and how he can get it off with out being on U.S. soil.

It didn't even cost him his life. He's too intelligent and clever to turn himself over. He told me he'd make a bigger impact than me writing books and talking shit. He told me how he'd hijack an airplane, well his Al-Queda henchman would.

He had a blueprint to take out the twin towers out in one day. Catch Americans off guard and see how the average working person runs in total terror. I'm translating that the message was loud and clear when he said it.

Osama knew that Katie Couric in a skirt is the only way I'll watch the Today Show. It's a turn-on for me. He said tape the Today Show that morning and watch his work. As the Americans ran for their lives he just sat back in his cave with a total snicker.

His work wasn't even done there. He had a couple of other targets but they were down in Washington D.C. the minute a Bush gets in office America is in war like the code of Jihad. Osama said he would be the mastermind and he trusted that Allah would protect him from evil.

When I wrote a chapter in Psychoville I mentioned how machetes were stolen out of my Echelon Glen Apt. Well they weren't. Osama told me he borrowed them he said he wanted to kill a Haitian female roach for me. He knows how I personally feel about them.

The hijacking took place and the Al-Queda soldiers tied up the pilots at the airport and stashed the captives in the airport closet. They said their last prayers before leaving this earth and permanently join Allah. That's when the plot was going down. I just listen and learned how to make a chapter to make of it.

America went into a total stage of shock. He tried to two-way me after the aftermath of the attack but the cell phones were shut down. The terror in America's eyes shows that he was out to strike first blood. He told me seeing the twin towers fall was like seeing you destroy a sandcastle.

Then there was the attack of the Pentagon. That was secondary because the World Trade Center was the big fish he really wanted to reel in. he wanted to blow it up back in 1993 but another groups of Arabs beat him to the punch. You thought that "Time to Die on the 11th" was the icing on the cake but it wasn't. I just took a pit stop in between books and started to chat up some ideas with Lucifer.

Now Lucifer is two waying me through my work to tell you how it was easily done. Then there were the pilots who crashed the planes in the building. They were depressed and didn't have nothing to live for anymore. If you got to go out take some people with you.

You take four planes to crash, three buildings, get planes slammed into it, the buildings was in two different cities, and it was rolled into one big plot. It went down that day and now America had to color code their terror alert.

The actions didn't end there. Tanya Menton is so dumb she got white out confused for anthrax. Osama was telling me to be careful when it involves the mail. They had some shit setup they were gonna send some anthrax to an anchor that worked for NBC nightly news.

America had fun taking control of Baghdad and hunting down Saddaam. They singled out Saddaam because they couldn't find bin Laden. Bin Laden told me he wanted to take the American Soldiers on a "Where's Waldo?" chase.

Our country would see him on the Al_Jezeera network and other videotapes to show that he's still alive and kicking. Are you guys really that stupid he didn't roll over and die from natural causes. He walks with a walking stick because he really sprained an ankle. He told me he's covered with the HMO plan.

He was voicing his opinion about his displeasure about a Bush being in the White House again. As soon as the Bush's fixed that election in Florida and he wants to show you how he felt. His thinking that results may vary and America needs to beg for mercy.

He didn't do that shit for shock value. He did it to show off his testosterone that he's not afraid to piss America off. His desire for revenge gave him the heavy motivation. He had this look in his eye that he was ready to go to war. They call it the worse attack on United States soil. Well the planning had to be direct and precise. You can't really translate what was said in Arabic. Americans don't speak in Arabic.

Many of us have issues with America that live in America but we may or may not react. It depends on what type of way that we're feeling. Drastic measures may lead to drastic results. The pilots if you didn't know were on suicide watch. They wanted to find a reason to leave the world. They wanted to go to a higher place just to rejoice with Allah. Then again they could be burning in hell like I will when I'm done writing this book.

When bin Laden was duckin' the U.S. troops he was playing hide and go seek just give him something to do. It was like playing tag and the troops were it. Osama told me if the troops would've found him he said he wouldn't be taken alive.

The day 9/11 took place it went down and I couldn't even reach him. The feds were tapping and listening to anything they could get a good lead on. Anything to stop the war on terrorism. Bush wants to sign these laws to start the war. I'm a citizen of the U.S. but I'm only speaking how it really was suppose to go down. Tears stream, people saw the horror, lives were sacrificed, and the Al-Queda forces were laughing.

bin Laden told me about the terrorist they're training to become killers. Everything you do ain't normal anymore because the planes in the building were just a sneak attack. The buildings collapsing with thousands of bodies going straight down in the rubble. It reached a point that American television can't even show that highlight of the planes going into the building. It bought back too many bad memories. Fuck having the funerals it was his time to get some souls off this earth.

Osama was pretty pissed how America just bullied on Iraq. For years tat shit was planned when Bush got in office he was going after Saddaam. The numbers 9/11 means the attack with Operation Desert Storm took place on 1/91. Remember that day because the numbers were flipped on the day the Islam would strike back.

Osama should've never told me because now the motherfuckers are gonna have me put under investigation about what I speak and what I write. Me and bin Laden speak so frequently that it scares the hell out of people that he told what's a coming and the color code alert will go at a higher level.

bin Laden told me he's in perfect health. He also said that he's not as pail as people think he is. That's the problem with the government that they're trying to study a tape to see if he's healthy. If you think he's sick he said send the get-well cards to me.

I try to convince him that America wasn't the enemy. I told him to join my alliance so we can kill the female Haitians. I told him if we send Bush a cheesecake he'll consider as a peace offering. I'm trying to build a good reputation for bin Laden to get him a green card.

About that situation why we dress like him for Halloween? Besides being Dirty Delgado they need an evil role model to look up to. It seems like he fits that mold.

America gets the planes blown up in their faces. A car bomb went off in Virginia somewhere. There are so many targets in America that has bin Laden licking his chops that makes him that much unpredictable. He tells me all he sees is blood in the water.

How are you gonna stop it if you don't know the next plot. Osama says he's in perfect health to know what he wants to do. As far as 9/11 was concerned he thought he gave the Americans exactly what they deserved.

I'm not the bad guy in this fuckin' country. I'm just the messenger who was given the instructions to tell you about bin Laden's issues. If it comes down for you fighting me, I'll just crash your plane into your building. Just because American troops ran out Hussein out of Iraq doesn't mean it's gonna happen to him. He'll be damned if he let something to go down like that.

Since he got America he just moved on to other shit. Bombing more people in other countries. Killing any journalist that tries to get any exclusive scoop on how the Al-Queda likes to handle their business. If you want to know the scoop and you think you got a hot story you won't get a chance to tell it.

I'm trying to get him to bomb places that don't want to publish me. He even gave me a guide on how to bomb and not get caught. He told me to go after every writer that I'm jealous of. I was taught by bin Laden how to brag when you make an impact like he did.

I even mixed up my white out with anthrax. When you open the envelope the anthrax will explode and spread on you like that monkey likes to spread the AIDS virus. He was telling me the world only got a tip of the iceberg.

Don't confuse me with John Walker Lindh and try to think I'm a traitor. I may be Wes Allen Muhammad but my first name isn't John. I said it and spoke it. I didn't write in Arab about what was just spoken. Anyway I hear another message coming from bin Laden once again and he's saying…

"Debug my brain and find out if you really want to know!"

Fight night at Jillian's

(CHAPTER TWENTY-SIX)

You know I was coming back to get you. What's up now muthafucker?! What's up now?! Time to die you fuckin' Eagles haters!

One fan! Two fans! Three fans! Four fans! Look at all the chaos this where the rowdiness begins. Chairs fly, girls cry, then the fuckin' fist fly, then guns come and all we're doing is trying to get the fuck out.

Andrew Robinson: It's Saturday night! It's me and the guys getting in a fight up in Jillian's. We get in a fight with a bunch of drunken Philadelphia Eagles fans.

What would Gracie think?

I don't give a fuck what Gracie think. I'm trying to get the fuck out of dodge and really trying to save my muthafuckin' self. The shit is getting crazy. It's getting wild! The Eagles fans try to start throwing punches me and the boys started swinging back. It had to all start because we got a table near the Eagles fans and voiced our displeasure about how we felt about the Eagles.

So what the fuckin' bums won the NFC title and went to the Super Bowl the fuckin' bums didn't win it anyway. It's enough satisfaction that the fans became so angry annoyed at us they tried to disrespect us by trying to spit in our direction.

There's six of us and Brian was the only one that was an Eagles' fan. He was down with us and if we went down he was going down with us. Oh shit more fans are charging. Mike Edge took two to three of them at a time. Corey is punching out Birdman. I'm right up near the entarnce door, it's a huge fight amongst us and there's six of us and it's just us against them.

"Crack! Bam! Pop!"

That's that's the sound of a chair going up against some nigga's head and he got cracked. Lamont picks on those senior citizens that play that "fly eagles fly" fight song and fuckin' beats them up with their own instruments. It's the sound of a rowdy time and we're on the middle of some shit. While we see that Andy Reid look-a-like as he gets involved in the mix.

Brian Liptrot: These muthafuckers are bugging! I just turn my back fo one minute and we already start buckwhylin. One minute it was all fun and all love than the Philly fans have to get disrespectful. Iwas sitting arouhnd until I saw Mike Edge swinging. That's my peeps and that's when I knew that I had to take his back.

I may be down with the Eagles but my boys are in a fight. When it's going down and they're in drama I got these niggas' backs. As soon as the drama got started in the section I thought you know who might've started off. He was nowhere around because he was probably up to no good anyway.

I see this plate full of lasagna and hit swoop in the face with it he was busy trying to put Andrew in a choke hold with his mascot wing. Come to think about it though it was funny how it got started because when the Eagle fans were cheering when their draft pick was next their was a section we reserved for us that hated the birds.

One of those rowdy Eagle fans had the nerve to start some shit. When Corey was booing the Eagles than a fan spit in his direction. Mike Edge asked what was the deal behind that and the fan tried to get really fired and start a fight. So a couple of fans jumped on his back and tried to take him down.

Well it's on now and we're fighting for our lives. We see the drunks coming back for more and the women grabbing their kids and trying to get to safety. I see beer mugs being smashed over my people's head, and chairs and objects being thrown like we're in World Wrestling Entertainment. This shit is the real thing and it's now being played out like a grown man's soap opera where we see men in tights going off.

T.V. reporters are catching this shit on film like they do to make it look like they're the paparazzi and to make it look like the anti-Eagles fans were the ones that started it. We don't see it that way and they think they can go around and disrespect anybody that ain't down with the Eagles. It's like Homey on living color and we don't play that shit.

I'm trying to run to my car and get my snubnose ready to set it off. Hopefully I'll be able to get to my car before something disaterous happens to any of my niggas.

Lamont: I'm flying down 295 tell me how far I am from Jillian's?!

Corey: It's where Franklin Mills Mall is at!

Lamont: Which end?

"Pow!"

Corey: I'm feeling pretty groggy. I need to collect my thoughts on what the fuck just happened.

Lamont: You O.K?!

Corey: I just fuckin' got sucker punched in the mouth.

Lamont: Are you dazed?!

Corey: I'm just rattled!

Lamont: I'm almost there!

Corey Palmer: Birdman kept shrieking as I kept hooking off on his skinny ass. God I hate the the Eagles and I'm doing something that I've been itching to do. It all had to start because Brian was sitting with us and he's our boy. When the Eagles were about to draft the fans got all rowdy and I was voicing my displeasure as me and the boys except Brian who was the only Eagle fan permitted to sit at our table.

Of course Brian had to call us a disgruntle 49ers fan. So when Brian stood up and cheered Mike Edge playfully grabbed him by wrapping a towel and act like he was choking them. Then of course an ignorant fan from Eagle nation had to be the one that started and punched Andrew in the face then that's when all hell broke loose and it was on and I'm fighting for my life.

They must've got us confused for one of the Minnesota Vikings' family members and they weren't gonna spit on us and have their way. We fight back and they think they're dealing with one of their own and we're not like any of those muthafuckers that they disrespect and think they'll get away with it.

Well it turned out to be a shootout and the fight was on and popping. I grabbed a mug and one of those Eagle fans that dresses up in that midnbight green and silver make-up tried to step to me but I grabbed a chair and smashed it over his head then he fell to the ground. Johnny and I began to stomp on him and another fna came out of nowhere and clothelined Tim in the back of the head and the fight looked like it was the WWE up in here.

Well in this match-up there wasn't nobody wearing a championship belt. Just a hate fest going on and how I began to show my distaste for the Eagles by disrespecting the fans. A Chair started flying and hit another fan in the face. I turn around and I see two fans trying to jump on Corey I had to run over with a broken leg off the chair and hit a fan in the back of the head.

The Eagles' players ran over to see what the commotion was about but then one guy got rowdy and started pulling a gun then I heard gunshots flying in the air and then niggas were running for their life. I heard Corey talking on the Nextel and trying to get Lamont to come out and give him some back-up and I knew that he was flying on his way down from Willingboro. The next miute I turn arond and I'm saying what the fuck is he doing?...

Kahlil: It's gotten real crazy then it ever has before. I been to Jillian's once and I wanted to check out the action and be the mean guy that spreads the blues to all the Eagle fans. Instead I was fuckin' trying to get Elizabeth's phone number so I was walking around Jillian's like I'm obsessed with the thought.

So the shit began to get hectic and I was minding my business then I saw Elizabeth and I tried to mack the girl. I wasn't paying any attenntion to what the hell is going on until I fuckin' saw a chair grazed me on top of the head.

Turned around and before I knew it I saw that Corey was getting into it and then I knew that duty called and I had to get in the middle of the excitement. I ran to Corey's car and grabbed the trusty nine iron because I don't go nowhere without it now. Came back and ran into Jillians and began to start playing psycho saying four swinging for niggas' heads.

During the melee I fuckin' saw the NFC Championship Trophy after I lost my trustee golfclub I had to grab that piece of shit that the Eagles won and break the bitch over somebody's head. The fun didn't stop there another attacker came at me with a chair. I ducked and slugged him in the face.

I saw that Mike Edge was handling his business by himself. Then I went over and punched a drunk guy in the face. Then I looked back and I saw more muthafuckers joined in the melee'. They saw the non-Eagle fans get started up like it was World War III up in this bitch and we were looking at it like it was us against the world.

When it comes to fighting I don't aim for that body shot and shit I'm aiming for punches to the face. All I know is that I fuckin' broke a couple of noses but I was sporting a fat lip. It came when I was thrown over the bartenders table by three Eagle fans.

Leave it to one of those sorry ass Eagles' fan to start some shit and now I got to be in some shit and I wanted to be up in Elizabeth. Instead I'm up in a fight. I see the Eagle players were nowhere to be found. It just got rowdy as a muthafucker and there were bullets flying and I got grazed with a broken glass coming close to my eyes and I'm fighting for my life and it's as crazy as I ever had a brush with death.

Before I knew it I ran in the gameroom and grabbed some objects that I could use as weapons. I ran back into the reastaurant and Brian and I were stomping a mudhole in a couple of dudes but before I knew it a guy hit me in the back of the head with a chair.

I fell to the ground and my head was throbbing and I knew that only the strong survive. It seems like the bad guy was about to meet his match as I got off the ground as I looked over a certain section I played dumb and saw that my golfclub was on the other side of the room, if I can get Brian to help me out to get over there.

I wish I could find Kenyetta and hop in our 2004 Nissan Altima where is she...

(A breeze goes by quickly)

The fuck it is her. Kenyetta is really trying to get the fuck out of dodge she's trying to save her own life she didn't give a fuck about the pom-poms. I can't say I blame her I be out to but it doesn't work like that. I see Elizabeth in the front seat and Kenyetta had driven the fuck off. I'm left to go back in and it's still my niggas fighting in their. I ran back in and as soon as I stepped inside the war zone I got slugged in the face.

I was so graugy that it left me in a daze. I passed out for a moment and I began to play possum. I was only left to resorting myself to trying to get out of the fight I got up and I saw Corey telling me to get of here and that they had it and I took his advice because I was falling out all over the place.

Before I even made it out three Eagle fans were stalking me hard and I made it out the door but I thought it was the end of me and before I knew it I turned around and fell on the sidewalk like I was a fuckin' drunk and just when I thought it was the end of me the fans ran back in the place all I know and remember that before I passed out, I saw my cousin Lamont shooting off his 38 and Jason came out with a loaded shotgun trying to blast the jokers that we were fighting.

Lamont Palmer: It's Saturday night and I'm here to finish it off. My brother Corey is in their getting his shit off and my cousin Kahlil is passed out on the ground. My best friend Brian is in their fighting too. I'm not in the mood for playing the knuckles game I'm into blasting niggas tonight. I had some chocolate weed and I'm still high but I'm focused to kill anybody violating my cousin and my brother.

It's so much shit going on this muthafucker that I just started blasting off in all directions. There's so much carnage that it's clear that I'm about to add a few to the casualty list and it's clear that Brian is the only Eagle fan that ain't getting killed.

It's clear that these guys have a war going up in this muthafucker and I'm out to get it started. I got the heart to kill somebody and some of these people fighting don't like the fact that they're facing life. Well it doesn't make a difference to me because my wife gets on my nerves anyway.

If I'm gonna go out and I have nothing to lose then I might as well make it worth my while. So nmow we can get a blood bath party going on in this muthafucker....

"So ones fot the money and two is to steal the show the third one is for that Andy Reid wannabe just to let you know!"

"Who's the muthafucker that knocked out my cousin Kahlil and is fighting with my brother?!

Before I got my hands on him Kahlil came out of nowhere and hit him in the back of the head with the sledgehammer.

One punch! Two punch! Three punch! Four punch!

All I see the carnage out this when we all made the fans take one for the team. Eagle fans are getting knocked out Lamont loading up the shotgun bodies all decked out. We laid the Eagles' fans out and somebody was gonna take a loss and it indirectly had to with the Philadelphia Eagles.

Still Standing

(Chapter Twenty-Six)

Mama there goes that man and he's at it again. He wants to talk about what vicious acts to say that book is about a bunch of bullshit that nobody wants to listen or hear. Touché I say and I'm here as long as I say that glass slipper and couch doesn't turn back into a pumpkin. Then again I had blonde hair but I don't think a blue gown and a glass slipper wouldn't look wouldn't look right on my foot but a size 11 Nike does it more for me.

Speaking of Nikes and feet sticking so many foot in peoples asses that I got so much shit on my foot it's like every time I walk I wound up stepping in dog shit. My foot isn't toilet papers for these fuckers it's to kick their asses and let you know I'm taking no prisoners. It's to let these idiots know that I take on all comers.

I caused so much mayhem and chaos in this hour that I'm far from finished. If you thought you were off the carousel when I bring out the next book we can ride the carousel again. So you best believe that I don't give a fuck whether the opinion is good or bad, I write for me. I'm not writing for two and I'm not expecting because you took me granted as a person but you will know who I am when it's all said and done.

It's not the end it's only the beginning of a journey, a trek, a path in this new phase of my life. I weathered it all God told me it has to be done that way. He says that vengeance is his but he gave me the green light and unleash a wrath on those who want to take me on and out. If my light is green there's no red in my sight. I went color blind because I can do and say shit and run with it all day.

I'm not gonna be perky and spunky using that rah rah chant. I heard all of that while the deck was stacked against me. Nobody gave me a chance but I should've realized everybody is gonna be against anthing you try and are gonna laugh when you try to do better. I should've learned to leap fearlessly knowing that my mom would be against whatever I tried.

The words that hit the Microsoft Word Document is like a way to have my voice on tape. How far will I go and deep into my details will I dig. Deep enough to pull a coffin from the ground or so deep like I reached inside your chest and had a live heart in my hand. Find that emotion that makes me stand out like a white girl sees me as the first black man they were ever attracted to.

It was written this way. I had to answer the bell. It may seem like I was knocked to the ground but I got back up. I take a standing eight and come out fighting for the next round. Best believe that I'm far from being washed up despite what these assholes think but there thoughts about me don't matter. I know who I am and I'm far from being a fart up in the wheel chair. Father time hasn't called me to hang up the keyboard.

My feet are firm and I got that swagger to excel. I'm past the handwriting and I'm no longer waiting to exhale. I'm trying to take it to my critics like Kobe did when he yammed on Yao. They said wouldn't happen but then again nobody believed they wanted to tune me out but from a bird's eye view they still wanted to be caught up in what the hell am I doing. It must be that important to give you some water buzz to take home and tell your family about me.

Ain't nothing to be scared of I remember this is my voice. I have so much shit to get out of me. I'm still donating my sales for cancer charities. Knowing those who know me that look down on me they're so stupid that think that I'll go and open a porn shop and be buried underneath Club Risque with my autograph pictures instead of doing something from the heart when these muthafuckers assumed I was thinking selfishly. I'm still shitting, whooping ass, and naming names not worrying about stupid shit like I'm a butterfly that makes no fuckin' sense because this ain't Halloween.

I put my foot down when I was finished with my ex-wife and I didn't do it to step on a roach. I can't get paid then the bitch had to go. I already knew it was a lie but when I got deeper into it and then there more lies I said fuck Kareen the bitch is good riddance and I can see myself kickin her coffin off the plane in midair if they flew her back to Jamaica to be buried.

Too bad my personality isn't one that you can understand so I fuckin' quit trying to please cocksuckers who know I'm on facebook and refuse to confirm me as a friend. 35 years of age and 11 years of writing not the dividends are paying off. I was destined for this moment no matter how far that goal looked realistic or was so far like a star you wanna touch that's falling.

They say I write garbage I beg to differ I write what I feel in my gut. These muthafuckers are saying that shit because they were too reluctant to speak what's the truth. I give you the FYI and I pull no punches because I let my dick speak louder that you hold under your breath. I'm not afraid to tell you or show you what I'm thinking because I'm no longer seen as the son Yvonne pushed out.

I just don't give a damn what's said and not to be said. The story needs to be told and I'm then being turned against because the truth hurts and it's more damning because it came from a person that they consider retarded or a lost cause. I'm the outsider and of course my story won't ever be given what's said.

Fuck what was said let's say I lay these haters to waste. Taking on different challengers and challenges from all level and maintain my record of consistency to perfection. Keep that record unblemished why I'm still public enemy number one and maintain that hunter's mentality even though I'm the one that's being hunted. I'm just as hungry as the next writer who wants to raise the bar after I'm done stating my claim.

I made this claim after the Ancora stint that I was far from finished. I guess I was worn and beat down and carrying infatuation just to impress somebody. Got over it and said I'm done sugarcoating shit and got back into what made me feared and hated. I use that as my fire and it energizes me when you demonstrate a group demonstration in regards to your issues with me. I got to admit that wicked part of me likes it that you can't fuckin' stand me.

I made a promise when I was writing back in 2004 that I never will let you down. My feet were weary and I had to put my issues out there. I had this build up and felt that scorpion venom was back in my tail and start stinging niggas like they're mice that need to be paralyzed before I sent you to that mouse hole in the sky. That was the writer and person that was missing for three years and I found that fire that makes me feel good when I'm up to no good.

Remember the writing parade never passed me by. I'm out to let you know I had to walk alone and it's fine I need alone time for me. Fuck these girls that enjoyed turning me down that got a high to say they got that last laugh because they wanted to walk around like there was no shit in their vaginas. You best believe that I'm being vicious and come up with a snarky counter to tell you that your bush isn't that clean like you advertise it to be.

While I'm out on that fuck you type of shit. You doubted me and I had no problem calling out muthafuckers that needed to be addressed. I'm not gonna let God handle them sometimes vengeance is my hands and I have no problem sending it and serving it cold. I got a menu of ways I want to serve it up and it's never game set and match against me. Like I told you I don't play checkers I play chess. Controlling the four center spaces on the board lets me control the board.

If I was that crazy why was whoopin' ass in Ancora in chess against orderlies and was crowned as the best in Ancora. I didn't declare myself as committed on my ends because muthafuckers in the court system saw me as a mere paycheck instead of a human being. A salary above minimum wage for them to be the crooked model citizens they claim to be. I'm not an animal you can throw in a zoo. I eat food like you do and I pass gas the same way you do.

I complained too much about what I was missing. Be happy with what was given to me and some aren't that fortunate like me. Cowboy up and lasso the down competition and you're enemies need to be grabbed by the horns and steered on their faces. It's like unzipping your pants pissing on them like a watergun at a carnival and the balloon blows up.

I don't know if a fuse was lit. I came out like a livewire that had an unexpected jolt and show what I can do. I can talk about whoever but always remember it still comes out and down to me. If you're a fan of mine then you were feeling me from the door. You know the man and I'm far from the writer that you were able to separate me from. At least you know who I really am. I never played masquerade and hid behind a mask being on some perpetrating shit.

While I'm on that separating the two shit at least you understand that I have a job to write and ain't afraid to back down what I say. What you confuse me as pestering I see it as being a speaker if I'm not a writer. It's doesn't need a seal by President Obama it came from my mouth and if the words have my stamp of approval it has the seal of "The Worlds Greatest Writer".

The bar is raised now and the only expectations I need to meet is mine. If it satisfy me then I did my job as a writer. I can sell one book and it won't make a difference what you think because I was cursed to speak what's on my mind. I said it and meant it it's too late to take it back especially if I email the chapter out.

Was it meant to be this way where this journey would take me to. If you talked shit on me than it's a must you're insulted back. As a bonus it brings me joy to gaslight you. I'm giving you the torture that you enjoyed giving out and karma is a bitch that you muthafuckers didn't mind giving out but you know you have to get it now.

I got these middle fingers that ain't afraid to be stuck up when my brain sends out the message to stick them up. They can be seen as a fuck you or an Italian salute no matter what you think it was addressed as a defense mechanism. I had to take a stand and I'm in a one man defense in a war and I enjoy three against one because to me you muthafuckers are outnumbered.

I can be dead and I still have a book out there. I won't be pulling out a Makaveli but my words will still be heard from the grave. I got so many chapters that weren't released that two books can come out and have the executor to my will still happy to carry on my name. There's no way to escape death because I know eventually I have to see that day when I pass. I'm here now and it's a gift because I'm in the present and "The Kahlil Weston Hour" is about to close the curtain and "The Wes Daddy Mack Hour" will have to be the next one to pick up when the hour closed out on.

It's the cliffhanger for Friday to leave you in suspense going into Monday. Do the hour all over again except on a different day but it's the same shit so you know that I'll be at it again. I'll still be raising hell and dropping jaws by the way I spoke on it. No need to cry because I'm at it's conclusion I have a new act and this episode is over pretty soon.

Let's be honest I don't fuckin' care if my days are short because I have no more honor for my mommy and kicked my dad's ashes because I'm seen me as the son that was denounced. Best believe this is how the path goes now. For better or worse and now denouncements was the death did us part.

What is the motivation for me to write well there's a number of reasons. It's like an escape where I can vent and belt out some chapters to state my issue and what I need to do to address it. I have a hatred, happiness, a rage, and mood to express and it'll come out and I'm not looking for any blessing to any opinions. If you're not afraid to write than you're not afraid to be read.

I'm a survivor and it was in my soul to be the last man standing. It was like I rose from the ashes with my balls in hands and the news broke like in a soap operas digest that I didn't die after all. It's like a revolving door when you think I'm at the end of my rope I find an extension cord like a cat can try to extend its 10th life. If cats have ten lives then there must be a five leaf clover in the grass.

If I had to write a chapter dissing me, I would be better crawling under a rock and let my closer friends tell me that I'm still a friend knowing that I was trumped and humbled. Crawling under a rock is like the rattlesnake that you are you're seeking refuge from the heat that was given by the words that I dished out and then there's a retreat to the cave. Those other snakes that ran to the cave after I was done with them are only taking your side because they want to boost your bruised ego.

Let me cut to chase while you were cutting cheese around the issue. You can throw me in the psychiatric hospitals, make fun of my crushes on red headed branch managers, accuse me of threats, house arrest me, be on some freeze out shit but understand that I'm not hiding those issues and you can't pull that skeleton out my closet because it's already been known. What ain't known is that to all those that was with Kahlil when he first went on this journey that I was given the green light to go.

I followed the yellow brick road to Author House now it's my turn to curse up a fuss. Kick up some dirt, hit above and below the belt, if I got to grab dirt from the ground to throw it in your eye if I need to then it'll be done. I understand that it's a duel and every man for himself but that's the competition to win the battle. Believe me I'm far from being over the hill and you have know idea how much effective I am in my 30's and I was too clueless when I was in my 20's.

"Here's the finale!"

I have to remember who I am now. I'm gonna be looked differently and I'm never going to get my due. Whatever comes next I'm ready for it and I go in it with effort and no fear of failure. I can take drama that you want to pepper me with but expect to get punched in the face right back at you. I already swam in the rain when you thought a rat was drowning. Any talks about my demise was greatly exaggerated.

It's not over! The company is dead. It all started with them and now it's beyond. I can earn a dollar a year and I make more than what that pissy little company makes now. Too bad you were too stupid to underestimate how much smarter than you make me out to be crazy.

Since they went to the company graveyard we've changed presidents. Everybody is on facebook now and it's a hit. A perpetrator I liked or had deep feelings for had a baby. My dad passed of cancer. I had a nasty divorce. My mom left me for dead. I can't appeal a grade but I can get expelled. Of course I'm still being exaggerated and the poster boy of being retarded.

Kissing Mika Brzezinski was my highlight of 2010. Who knows what I might be up to in 2011. I'm not gonna be twittering and facebooking all my moves. You say your tuned out but from a birds eye view you know you're tuned in. What's that buzz about that you heard about what I've done now. I still like that forty something redhead branch manager that works in TD Bank in Voorhees, New Jersey.

If it wasn't the talk with the redhead I would've hated to see where my state of mind was really at. I would've picked up a burglary charge, cut up some clothes, smashed up a GPS, and anything else in that fuckin house. It would've been a rampage and I would've left fingerprints around the crime scene and you can match them up because I want to be identified as the Dali that did art of terror.

I'm still running my mouth about Nancy Pelosi is one how piece of ass in her 70's. I really didn't fuckin' lose my mind when I said it. What seems as weird to you may seem cute to me and flattering to her. So you best believe when I return back to the realm of writing you know I'll be promoting porn and proud to admit it.

No need to cry about the respect I get because its irrelevant now. I guess I'll have a few more friends on Facebook who's gonna come out the woodwork now. They had amnesia about who I was when you knew me but now all of a sudden now I'm the long lost best friend that went to grade school with you and now your phoniness is out now.

I exhausted ideas the tank is empty. No my engine didn't die. I had to take a pitstop. I didn't pull a Dale Earnhardt and crash into the wall. It's time to break and get ready for the one. The only idea I have now is to outdue this one. I do have a promise to you......

I promise to bring my "A" game in all books I bring out beyond. Life is too short not to serve my purpose. All my opponents can bring their "A" game but I'm so far ahead of you that I see it as your "B" or "C" game and that's how I see it. I ain't no little boy, an animal, and I'm far from a fly on the window. I'm the elephant in the room; you best believe I'm here to stay.

Anxiety Attack

(Bonus Chapter)

How in the hell did I ever get so crazy and complicated? Get these racy thoughts that make me want to be a psychopath? Watch a soap opera and watch a baby get passed off as someone else's. Witness the paternity test in a storyline that you thought this person couldn't be the mother or the father. It's like watching Erica Kane hop into the bed with a man half her age and get an attraction attack.

It's in the world soaps and it's fictional. I'm trying to be the poster boy for writer's wrath or am I the asshole who wants to stick his dick in Krystle Tucci's ass. Another one of my issues that I had to attack on the run like T-Mobile on the go talking about her mom's ass just ain't what it use to be.

I have this black lady that is a tock ticker. To think she pushed me out her vagina. I guess my days will be shorter because I didn't honor a commandment. So much damage that was caused and my aunt has to come to the realization that the bitch is dead to me like my father is in his urn. To all y'all that think that I'm an asshole for talking about it you can thank Yvonne for driving me to this decision.

They wanna say that's my mommy well I beg to differ. I'm no longer a mama's boy like some people who are grown ass men that let their mommies fight their battles and too much of a vagina with a bush to come out of his house. It has me snapping that makes me hold on to a grudge five or ten years down the line.

When you're serial and psycho you run around with hoodies and deadly weapons to carry out the plot. It thickens more once you do the deed and then you add subplots to your details. You're psyche is at a state of alert so sleep with one eye open and best believe that it's gonna go down. I'm out to dish out consequences and introduce you to my friend with the arrow shaped tail down in hell.

Like any sinister person who writes I get theses twisted plans to get what I need to rule. I have wicked intentions to do it illegally. Anybody who tries to be the white knight that tries to foil my evil plot you know the rule book goes out the door. I'm all about felonies and having a big laugh like "The Joker".

I could be on some sick shit and find a squirrel as roadkill on a road and take him up and boil him up fur and all and place him on a platter like it's rabbit meat or the child that was intrigued to see John the Baptist head on a platter. I'm getting sicko stage like Reagan was shot because somebody wanted Jody Foster's attention. Taking meds and Ritalin will not stop be from causing these demonic acts. I wonder if I burn in hell will I be able to wear Bermuda shorts and get some sun and a tan.

I'm number one with a bullet and I'm as passionate about my thoughts in writing like an intense Lebron James who hates giving up easy baskets. I get these anxiety aggressions that makes me say…

"World's Greatest Writer talking crazy say what!"

I can lie about shit to get my own reality show. Be on some my son is in the balloon to get a reality show just like my ex-wife lied to me totally in my 18 months of marriage. Call her a bitch because in my eyes I see her as. I swore I saw John Shuck running around with a Hannah Montana wig on his head.

Delgado is talking real dirty. Is it Wes just being wicked? Jamal is just being a jerk off. Kahlil is too creepy like a spiderweb to be trusted. It seems like the stories about me go on like a dirty tabloid. I'll hear that I slept with somebody's sister and the father will be in front of them when I allegedly say it.

I got the swagger of a psycho who loves wiping blood on the victim that I laid to rest. I get these happy go lucky rushes like I stood over a dead body that I took pride in taking their life. It's like doing a wardance in celebration like I made a sacrifice but I'm so proud of my work. I can take so many meds and it won't control my desire of causing carnage and I'm possessed by the demon who's requesting me to do these dastardly acts.

So many weapons to choose and it's so hard to decide. It's like having an Xbox 360 in front of you and having fucking picking the game you want to play. I'm playing a deadly game and it involves who I want to kill tonight. I have that thought of taking another life and I do it with no remorse. All that depressant is doing is taking me to a darker state and calling for me to have that blood on my hand.

That blood on the hand is like moisturizer or lotion. It doesn't make my skin feel dry. I kill people and I don't cut chickens head off it doesn't give me a thrill seeing them get that last nerve out of them. You can call me a name and I'll laugh sadistically plotting on how to get you back.

Boy am I so gone like Kelly Clarkson sung in her song. I say it but without love and no Justin involved in this sequence. Give me another porn star kiss and those nympho craves subside because I'm star struck by being in their presence. This is my real life of Californication because having sex once a day ain't enough I'm still watching porn like having some vagina still isn't enough.

I just throw on the tantrum fits and get into these sadistic modes. You better tackle me inject me with sedatives and having me all woozy with a wagging tongue. Tie me down with those big rubber straps and make sure I'm completely out of it if you want me not to commit anymore sinful acts. I kicked so much ass spit on you now I'm being contained like the man in the iron mask.

Looking at my hands not committing something negative is making them twitch. I can't run around naked with a watergun and scream how much I love getting soaked like bullets bounce off of Superman. I get a severely twisted when I can run loose and verbally attack you but I have more sinister plans that'll make you more humble.

Give me a dose of depakotb I got ADHD so there's no way I can be bipolar. Get these deadly acts out my system but it ain't enough because it turns my stomach in knots. I don't need a bottle of vodka to get me started on going crazy mode. I may walk around with a dust mask, have a jheri curl wig on and you confuse for the superstar that overdosed in his house. Then again I'm the pop star that never grew up and still wanted to live my childhood until I died at age 50.

You better pull out the jacket and have the strait on standby. Better yet get the tranquilizer darts and shoot me like I'm an animal running around the city on the loose. Keep me locked in the Holly Ward but then again I don't want to take the meds because they'll make me want to be happy and play with construction paper and taste paste.

I can get myself a big ass pot and boil your body until your skin and your flesh is boiled off like when you boil the carcass of a chicken and make a broth out of it. Find a pitbull that was sacrificed from dogfighting and couldn't survive then sell his body off to the Chinese and get his flesh confused for pork fried rice. It's like you're in 10th grade biology and you have to dissect the animal. Looking nasty because it's dead but dissect but cut it open and impressed with how the organs are so neatly in place.

I can commit a murder so fast that Usain Bolt wouldn't have made it to 100 yards before I'm all said and done. Grab your face with the blade and put a bloody smile on your face as if you're the joker on "The Dark Knight". It ain't a scar it's a sign to let you know that you smile at the world. Just put that shit on broadcast and make you say some shit I want you to say before I go on another murder spree. Setting up traps to lure you in and be smart about how they way I want to map it out.

After I'm done humiliating you then shake the camera up on the tube so they wonder what hell is going on now. It's a deadly game that I'm playing and understand this I'm the predator. When I'm done with the deadly torture hang you from somebody's window when they open the blind and let them know this ain't hangmen but the body hanging on your window gives you another blind or curtain.

Is my mind just filled with poison and I just don't know any better. Like the bitch that was made with one rib that let the serpent tempt her to eat fruit that was forbidden before thorns were thrown all around the garden. In some view I sprouted a tail out that made me Satan's offspring and breath and carry a pitchfork around stabbing people in the ass with the forks.

Is this what crazy people do? Are their brains so scrambled and irrational? Irregularly thrown off and are seen as better father figures and significant others and they kidnap babies and throw em' over the bridge. Before the inevitable happens they should've taken them as patients in Ancora. Then they say I'm the one with the loose screws.

I get these panic attacks that it makes me sort of lash out. I refuse to take the meds and daring the orderlies to pin me down and inject me with the lethal doses I'm entitled to. They tell me to take them and I milk the deadline and refuse. I have the ward team at my demand because I'm irrationally crazy.

You give me a bargaining chip and you meet my demands. I don't take the meds to prove a point. Then again I have the rope stashed under my bed because I might strangle someone in the ward. Not killing someone is making that anxiety that much stronger. It's in me to kill somebody and I'm going crazy if I don't.

Shooting somebody doesn't do it for me. I want it to be more violent than that. Busting a gun is too simple and all the rappers have said it in their raps. I'd rather wear a hood and have a big ass knife behind my back like I had crossed fingers. It's like when I'm done having sex I'm still not satisfied. Being that type of nymphomaniac gives me same desires as a criminal.

I was put in a corner and I had to come out swinging. That knife in my hand makes me that much more deadly if I find the right person to cut. Slicing arteries, cutting out the hearts, and that rush I feel feeling it beat in my hand. The heart is getting its last beat like a chicken does when their heads get chopped off. It's just getting that last nerve out of it.

I have this thing where I want to get dirty and nasty. Doing that shit is better than ripping intestines out of their bodies. That shit is so fucking good. Feeling those organs are all squishy I don't know if I wanna squeeze and watch them mush up it's too graphic that makes you wanna throw up like you dissected shit and you had lunch after science.

Having these anxiety moods is making act like "Sybil". I start going crazy and I'm talking to myself. I hear the crown clapping in my mind like Suzanne Stone Morretto was picturing herself in when Nicole was portraying her in "To Die For". Why have somebody do my dirty work and I love the blood on my hands. It gives me that excitement like a kid when he gets to play with his play-doe.

Speaking of play-doe I can sculpture people I don't like and make voodoo dolls and imagine bad things to happen with them. Stick a sewing pin in their butts and the next minute they have hemorrhoid attacks. It didn't come from straining and taking a shit. While I'm on the subject don't think using suppositories is going to fight off that pain.

I'm fixing a hex on them like I'm a witch doctor. Mama there goes that man as he places curses on his enemies like the Bambino did in Boston for 86 years. Do a war dance like the Crazy Horse blood that runs inside my body that makes me think I'm in Menoken, South Dakota. I still see myself as a Weston first and never as a Menoken.

While I'm on that Indian talk I guess in "The Kahlil Weston Hour" I talked so reckless that I was on the warpath. Hunting down the opposition with a bow and arrow and my tomahawk and scalping them down. After awhile chasing people naked with a chainsaw gets too tired that I need to come up with fresher ideas. I guess when I kill someone I can go and do that Indian wardance.

All this time I was talking to you with the intent to kill by having a scalpel behind my back. Stabbing up a squirrel in a park doesn't do it much for me. I get chills down my spine when I see them get ran over and they're stiff on their back. Stabbing a squirrel like crazy is like carving a pumpkin on Halloween.

This ain't an April Fool's joke. When I told you I was going to get published all you did was laugh. I guess I was taken serious as Obama was when he said he was running for President of the United States.

"It ain't a laughing matter now!"

I guess getting names out my system is better but getting sued is a lot better because it got their attention enough to piss em' off. If you tink you got the last laugh you best believe that if I decide to slam you in a chapter you're in my torture chamber. Ten pages of intense of a total cussing out and black humor with the punchline to let the reader go…

"Awww! Damn! Look what he said!"

That's how it's going down when I'm locked into getting that aggression out of me. You couldn't imagine the build up I feel when I'm out to crush you. All that anxiety came from when you gave it out but you couldn't take it. Don't get nervous because you ain't built to shoot your mouth off. If I had a gun in your mouth then all of a sudden it's like you're sucking dick to save your life.

I don't don a hockey mask I make sure this is the last face that you see. You best believe that when it's time to move on down below and you're wearing black down there I have more mayhem and chaos to unleash. Sex is hot and heavy down there and I can get my therapy on down there. I don't need a clinic to cure that addiction.

My hand is twitching because it's itching to do something that'll keep me in sin. I write the books because I'm out to bludgeon the competition and going rogue will be bleeding once I hunt down the opposition. I'll just slice em up with a knife like when I cut my hand intentionally. I feel like I was lost in the mix and nobody wants to pay attention to what I have to say.

All the medication I been taking is making me feel green. I feel like I'm in one of those zones where I spas out and I feel like I'm the son of American Psycho. Give me a thyroid mixed with arm and hammer in my elixir and I'm running crazy like I'm a thoroughbred. I'm so out of it every woman I see I have this crazy imagination that they're walking around in public with just a bra and thong on and nothing else.

Am I singing a song how I want my mullet back? I went back to black hair because I'm mourning that I'm no longer a blonde. Have I gone that nutty that I'm a squirrel that's being chased by nuts that but I'm seeing this in my nightmare. It's like waking up in a cold sweat did I daze off that I had imaginations that I have somebody's blood in my hand.

Isn't it funny how I went off the deep end? I should've wore swimming in the rain. Should I have kissed my father's ashes after he was cremated? Should I unleash on this Haitian Bitch that I can't fuckin' stand! Not to mention the bitch she has as a Facebook friend who has the ugly blonde hair that makes her look like little boy blue. Or should I call out that Philadelphia Eagles cheerleader who sees herself as a different shade because she sold out bigger than I'm accused of.

Now I'm to a point that I have a thing for the red headed milf who's built like the Ferrari that I dreamed of driving. It makes my teeth itch like so bad like I need the Listerine to fight that gingivitis and it has me going nuts. If I had a one hour dinner date with her I guarantee that she's signing divorce papers by the 59th minute. Is it my imagination I like to see her in a ponytail wearing a cheerleaders uniform and cheering me on while I commit another felony knowing I got a few more in mylifetime before it's all said and done.

As twisted as my mind gets it was subliminally calculated with so much mayhem to stir up that I'm energized and to take the title that belongs to me. I already my throne is the hotseat I wouldn't see it no other way. It was reserved for me because I chose it that way. It reminds of home when I down in hell. I have circles reserved for people that I lay waste to. Choosing them is like picking which duck in a pond I want to aim the shotgun at.

I'm so lost like a homeless stray. I made a statement about my mom being an asshole. I made the comment another reason why people can slam me and say that I'm a retard. Like half these people don't know how to play basketball but the make baby calls that makes me rename it as divaball. I also have a hit list of all the writers that I wanna kill so I can make everybody read my fuckin' book.

"I'M DONE!"

About the Author

Kahlil Weston is the author who bring a sharp wit and edge in this bold and brass combination of autobiographical and fictional world in the ways I see it and view as the world is about to step into the crazy world in the book and the life of being Kahlil Weston.

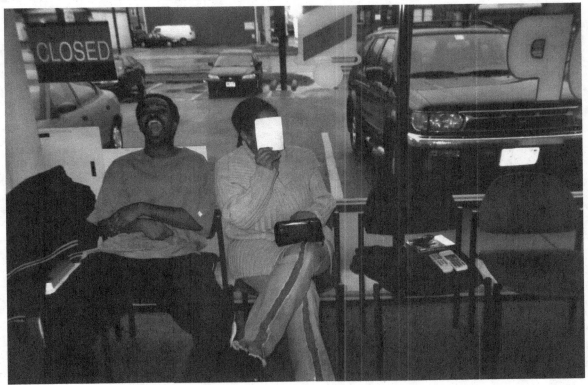

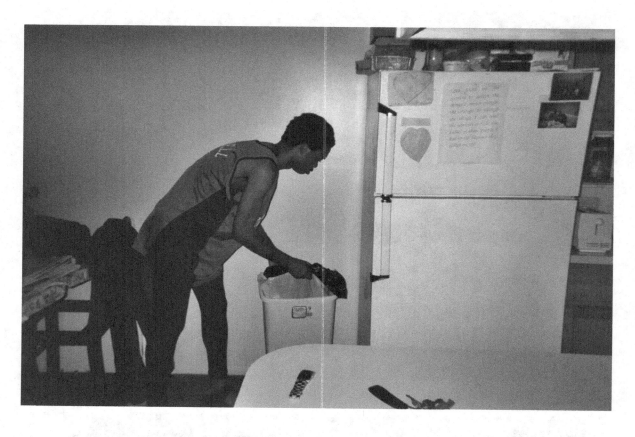